Managing Volunteers

Managing Volunteers

How to Maximize Your Most Valuable Resource

Nancy Sakaduski

 PRAEGER

AN IMPRINT OF ABC-CLIO, LLC
Santa Barbara, California • Denver, Colorado • Oxford, England

Library of Congress Cataloging-in-Publication Data

Day, Nancy.
   Managing volunteers : how to maximize your most valuable resource / Nancy Sakaduski.
     pages cm
   Includes bibliographical references and index.
   ISBN 978–1–4408–0364–2 (hardcopy : alk. paper) — ISBN 978–1–4408–0365–9 (ebook)
1. Volunteers. 2. Voluntarism—Management. I. Title.
HN49.V64D39   2013
302′.14—dc23   2012045038

ISBN: 978–1–4408–0364–2
EISBN: 978–1–4408–0365–9

17 16 15 14 13   1 2 3 4 5

This book is also available on the World Wide Web as an eBook.
Visit www.abc-clio.com for details.

Praeger
An Imprint of ABC-CLIO, LLC

ABC-CLIO, LLC
130 Cremona Drive, P.O. Box 1911
Santa Barbara, California 93116-1911

This book is printed on acid-free paper ∞

Manufactured in the United States of America

To the men in my life: Joe, Matt, and Dad

If you want to build a ship, don't drum up people together to collect wood and don't assign them tasks and work, but rather teach them to long for the endless immensity of the sea.

—Antoine de Saint-Exupery

Contents

Acknowledgments

Thank you to Ronna Charles Branch, UPS Global Reputation Management PR Supervisor; Maureen K. Eccleston, Director, Volunteer Maryland; Susan Ellis, President of Energize, Inc.; Dan Gabor, Regional Field Director, Organizing for America PA; Tony Goodrow, Founder of Volunteer[2]; Kory Hitchens, Insurance Advisor, Bramhall Hitchen Insurance; Meghan Kaskoun, Volunteer Manager, Aronoff Center for the Arts, Cincinnati Arts Association; Mary Pat Knauss, Board President, Wings for Success; Tia Milne, Volunteer Manager, Northern Illinois Food Bank, Geneva, Illinois; Cynthia Myers, Facilitator of the Family Council at Ingleside at King Farm in Rockville, Maryland; Lynn Spreadbury, Partner Engagement Manager, Save the Children; Jim Starr, Vice President of Volunteer Management, American Red Cross; and Mary Vaughan, Volunteer Coordinator for the MobileMed ministry at the Episcopal Church of the Ascension, Gaithersburg, Maryland, for providing valuable insights and advice. Thanks to Joe Sakaduski and Bob Day for their support, editorial assistance, and suggestions.

Introduction

> People assume ... if you've been a volunteer you can manage volunteers ... That's like saying "I've had brain surgery, so I can do brain surgery."
>
> —Susan J. Ellis, President of Energize, Inc., a training, consulting, and publishing firm that specializes in volunteerism[1]

Managing volunteers isn't brain surgery, but it isn't so easy that you can succeed just by using common sense either. Some people find themselves thrust into volunteer management with no training or preparation, like the young man who came to Susan Ellis for help after he was asked to coordinate the massive numbers of volunteers streaming into the Jacob Javits Center in New York City after the terrorist attacks of September 11, 2001. (He had just gotten his MBA but knew nothing about managing volunteers.) Other people have managed volunteers for years but want to improve their effectiveness.

Whether you are an experienced manager or new to the job, there are always different techniques to learn, tips to try, and ideas to consider. This book is intended as a broad introduction to the various aspects of managing volunteers. Volunteer management is an enormous subject, with many aspects and points of view. So consider this a place to start your journey, not the destination.

Volunteerism is a huge part of society, and volunteers play a critical role in communities around the world. A wide variety of organizations provide essential services with the help of volunteers. Some organizations also have paid staff, while others are run entirely by volunteers. Organizations may engage volunteers sporadically or on an ongoing basis.

The person who manages volunteers may be called the volunteer leader, volunteer manager, director of volunteers, volunteer coordinator, or some other term. The position may be paid or unpaid, may be full time or part time, and may report to a president, administrator, executive director, or board of directors. In small organizations, one person may serve as both executive director and volunteer manager, or volunteer management may be assigned to a paid staff member as an additional responsibility. The manager may work with a group of volunteers within the organization's own program or coordinate with agencies that supply volunteers to the community.

It is difficult to determine the exact number of volunteers worldwide, as most governments do not keep statistics on unpaid workers. A Johns Hopkins University study conducted in 37 countries determined the number of full-time equivalent volunteers was approximately 140 million people. If that number of people were the population of a country, the country would rank in the top 10 (above Japan).[2] A Eurobarometer survey conducted in 2006 found that three out of 10 Europeans claim to be active in a voluntary capacity (in an area of almost 500 million citizens).[3]

In the United States, volunteers served 8.1 billion hours in 2010, valued at an estimated $173 billion.[4] More than a quarter of all Americans over age 16 perform volunteer work for an organization at some point during the year.[5] While budgets have shrunk and government funding has been cut, the number of people who volunteer has remained relatively constant; volunteers are helping bridge the gap in a world of increasing need and dwindling resources.

Unfortunately, the mesh between the needs of organizations and the desires of volunteers is not always ideal. A study conducted in Canada identified gaps between what volunteers are looking for and how organizations engage volunteers. The primary gaps identified by the research were:

- Many people are looking for group activities, but few organizations have the capacity to offer them.
- Many volunteers have professional skills, but they may be looking for volunteer tasks that involve something different from their work life.
- Organizations are expected to clearly define the roles and boundaries of volunteers, but many volunteers want the flexibility to determine what they will do (i.e., create their own volunteer opportunity).

- Many organizations want long-term commitment, but many more volunteers are looking for shorter-term opportunities.

- Many organizations focus on what they need but besides helping others, many volunteers come with their own goals to be met.[6]

How well volunteers are managed makes a big difference in the success of the organization. Unfortunately, however, many organizations do not invest in the management of their volunteer programs. In the United States, about one-third of paid staff volunteer coordinators have never had "any formal training in volunteer administration, such as coursework, workshops, or attendance at conferences that focus on volunteer management."[7] Yet knowledge and use of good volunteer management practices affects how effectively a manager of volunteers runs the program. A 2003 survey on volunteer management by the Urban Institute found that organizations that had adopted more volunteer management practices had higher net benefits than organizations that had adopted fewer. The survey also found that organizations with an identifiable volunteer coordinator had higher net benefits than organizations without a coordinator. It didn't even matter much if the coordinator was paid or unpaid. What mattered was the time devoted to managing the volunteers and the use of good practices in managing them.[8]

The challenge is to develop a program that is comprised of skilled, energized, and committed volunteers who work in partnership with board volunteers, paid staff members, and clients to further the goals of the organization—a program in which volunteers give the organization added skills and capabilities, and enable the organization to provide more services, reach more constituents, and have a bigger impact. In this setting, volunteer efforts are treated as one of the valuable resources (like financial donations and grants) necessary for the organization's success.

I hope this book will provide realistic examples, useful information, and practical advice that will help you do your job more effectively and improve the impact of your organization's volunteer program. Pay particular attention to the advice given by the professionals I interviewed, as their experiences can save you time and trouble.

Educate yourself about your profession. Read, use the resources in Chapter 10, and go online. You will find a wealth of information that will save you wasted effort and prevent you from making some of the common mistakes.

I also encourage you to reach out to professional organizations, networking information exchanges, and other nonprofit organizations and agencies in your area. You will find that volunteer managers are very will-ing to share what has worked (and not worked) for them, as they have likely faced a similar problem at one point or another.

Above all, remember that volunteers are giving you the most valuable thing they have: time. It's up to you to spend that donation efficiently and effectively.

THE 10 COMMANDMENTS OF GOOD VOLUNTEER MANAGEMENT

1. *Do unto volunteers as you would have them do unto you.* Treat volunteers with respect and courtesy, and make them an essential, valued, and integrated part of the organization.

2. *Thou shalt not kill enthusiasm.* Remember the "constructive" in "constructive criticism" and make sure positive comments outnumber the negatives. Criticize quietly and privately. Understand your volunteers' motivations and feed them.

3. *Thou shalt not steal ideas.* Give credit where credit is due.

4. *Thou shalt not squander volunteers' time, for that is an abomination.* Make the best use you can of every ounce of volunteer effort. Making sure the volunteers' donation (of time) is well spent ensures their satisfaction and the program's efficacy.

5. *Thou shalt not forget that there is more than one way to skin a cat.* Different people have different ways of doing things. Allow for individuality, as long as the goal is accomplished in an acceptable manner.

6. *Thou shalt honor thy volunteers and convey gifts of kindness unto them.* Recognize your volunteers and show thanks as often as possible.

7. *Thou shalt not bear false witness.* Be honest with your volunteers; admit mistakes and never cover up. When there is a problem, describe the situation clearly and explain what the organization is doing to correct it.

8. *Thou shalt watch over thy volunteers, keeping them into order.* Take the time to match volunteers to tasks that make good use of their knowledge, skills, and desires. Monitor their work but allow them autonomy within guidelines. Address any problems quickly.

9. *Thou shalt give rest to those who labor.* Make sure your volunteers have down time; allow for fun and avoid burnout.

10. *Thou shalt seek flexibility.* Remember that people have lives, families, jobs, hobbies, athletic endeavors, school, and all the obligations that go along with those activities. Allow volunteers to contribute when and where they can, and show gratitude for whatever time they are able to donate.

CHAPTER 1

Where to Start

Begin at the beginning and go on till you come to the end; then stop.
—The King to the White Rabbit, in *Alice in Wonderland*
by Lewis Carroll

THE PLAN

As Aristotle said: "A job well begun is half done." This is excellent advice, particularly from such an early volunteer organizer (Aristotle's school was managed by the students). Preparation is half the battle with any job, and that is certainly true when it comes to developing a successful volunteer program.

Start with a plan. The organization may already have a long-range strategic plan or an annual operating plan (or both). You may also have a volunteer plan. Or, you may have some combination of these kinds of plans. If not, you will want to develop one. As the variously attributed quote goes: "Failing to plan is planning to fail."

A plan forces you to assess constituency needs, recognize organizational strengths and weaknesses, set goals, determine what resources (including volunteers) are needed, address needs for infrastructure such as policies and procedures, establish deadlines, and specify who will do what. A plan also provides a way to measure progress and evaluate results. Without a plan, you are recruiting soldiers to fight a war that hasn't been determined. Do you need desert fighters or sailors? Pilots or communication technicians? Soldiers who can march and carry a rifle or linguists who can translate documents into another language? Generalists or specialists? How are your soldiers to be deployed and in what numbers? As in war, the name of the game in creating an effective workforce is not only amassing a large army, but also identifying and training a strategic combination of tactical fighters.

Having a good plan is critical to managing and growing the organization. "We wouldn't be able to do it without planning" says Lynn Spreadbury, Partner Engagement Manager for Save the Children, an organization that has programs in more than 120 countries, including the United States. "It could be something as simple as perhaps we have funding to go ahead and build a new school. Well if we were to go externally and hire a company to build that school for us, but were to find out a month later we had a team of volunteers coming from the States that could have helped build that school and assisted or provided reduced labor ... then obviously [we] are out of sync."[1]

Mary Pat Knauss, Board President of Wings for Success, a much smaller organization with just 40 volunteers, says that they use both a three-year strategic plan and an annual operating plan. "What that has done is brought incredible focus to the organization for decision-making and for moving forward within the mission along a path ... It's allowed us to move forward much more quickly than I think the organization would have otherwise." Knauss says they review their annual goals monthly at the board meeting and review the strategic goals quarterly. "We're in our third year of implementation and during that three-year period we've doubled the number of clients we've served and we've grown our financial resources three-fold."[2]

I strongly encourage you to make planning a cooperative process, with input from the paid staff, board members, and other volunteers. This ensures shared ownership and increases the chances that the groups will work together to achieve common goals.

Everyone, from the executive level on down, should understand, appreciate, and support the volunteer workforce, and that integration should be apparent in the strategic plan. Susan Ellis of Energize, Inc. says, "Even if an organization has a volunteer coordinator ... that does not mean that the executive level of that organization is off the hook for thinking about volunteers, and all too often that is what happens."[3] The plan should represent a shared vision of the mission of the organization, including how both paid staff and volunteers contribute to the successful achievement of the organization's goals.

Before starting to create a strategic plan, the key players should get into a tiny metaphorical helicopter and fly up, up, up, above the day-to-day running of the organization. Navigating carefully around the valley of "that's the way we've always done it" and over the "it can't be done" hills, the helicopter's passengers should gaze down and examine both where the organization is and where it would like to be. Only from this vantage point can one see the numerous roads, paths, and pitfalls between the two. The routes chosen will depend upon the needs of the constituency the organization serves, the mission of the organization, and the resources the organization can bring to bear.

Where is the organization now? This question may be tougher to answer than you think. For one thing, it depends on who you ask. The perceptions of paid staff, board members, front-line volunteers, constituents, and the general public may be quite different. The organization's current position includes its financial health, image and visibility in the community, services provided, use of resources (human and financial), and impact.

A key part of the planning process is assessing the needs of the constituency the organization serves (or plans to serve). A needs assessment should also include input from the paid staff. Needs assessments can be done through surveys, interviews, focus groups, demographic research, and observation. What are the community's needs? How are needs currently being met (or not met)? What more could be done given the necessary resources?

The plan should be consistent with the mission of the organization and its core values. Everyone in the volunteer program should know what the mission is, and everything the group does should forward that mission. A good mission statement is concise, clear, and specific.

Here are a few examples:

- "Back on My Feet is a nonprofit organization that promotes the self-sufficiency of those experiencing homelessness by engaging them in running as a means to build confidence, strength and self-esteem."[4]
- "The Human Rights Campaign advocates on behalf of LGBT [lesbian, gay, bisexual, and transgender] Americans, mobilizes grassroots actions in diverse communities, invests strategically to elect fair-minded individuals to office and educates the public about LGBT issues."[5]
- "The American Society of Nephrology leads the fight against kidney disease by educating health professionals, sharing new knowledge, advancing research, and advocating the highest quality care for patients."[6]

Some organizations also create a vision statement, which is a view toward the future of where the organization would like to be. A vision statement is a way of defining how the organization will change over time and may be philosophical or inspirational. Here is an example of a vision statement: "The vision for the Homeless Assistance Leadership Organization (HALO) is that all homeless individuals and families in Racine County will be provided emergency food, clothing, shelter, transitional and permanent housing, and supportive services through a collaborative structure that effectively coordinates services, shares information, increases funding and eliminates duplication and gaps in services."[7]

Core values are another important consideration. Knauss says her organization's core values make it easy for her to attract and keep volunteers at Wings for Success and help explain why they are effective as an organization. "It's those values that really guide how we treat each other in the organization and how we treat our clients in terms of respect for the individual ... the power of a woman to make a better life for herself. It really sets the tone for us as an organization."[8] Core values govern how an organization conducts its business, and cover its treatment of paid staff, volunteers, constituents, and the general public. Here are the core values of Wings for Success:

- All women have the capacity to be successful in the workplace.
- A person's image affects one's job, salary, and possible promotions.
- Self-esteem is critical to the health and well-being of women.
- Every person deserves to be treated with dignity, compassion, and respect.
- Economic security, health, and education are fundamental human rights.[9]

Once the needs have been assessed and a clear mission statement has been created, conduct a strengths, weaknesses, opportunities, and threats (SWOT) analysis. Strengths and weaknesses are internal factors such as communication, infrastructure, and resources. Opportunities and threats are external factors such as demographic trends, economic fluctuations, and changes in funding. A SWOT analysis can help bring to light factors (both positive and negative) that should be addressed in the plan.

You should now have enough information to develop goals and objectives. These terms are often used interchangeably, but most people use "goals" to mean long-term outcomes and "objectives" to mean short-term (within a year) outcomes. Objectives also tend to be narrow in focus and measurable.

Once the goals and objectives are in place, you can create the strategies and tactics—the road map—for how the organization will get from where it is to where it wants to be. Each objective should be supported by one or more strategies, and each strategy should include one or more tactics that describe the who, what, where, how, and when of implementing that strategy.

Remember to assign responsibility and timing (ideally a specific date) for each task. Note that people assigned the responsibility can be paid staff, board members, committees, individual volunteers, or any combination.

Volunteer activities should be woven into the plan, not treated as a separate element. As you see where volunteers fit into the goals and objectives for the organization, you will better know what capabilities you need, when you need them, and who might provide them, which can help you direct your recruiting efforts.

There are entire books on strategic planning, but the basics of a good plan are universal: to set goals and objectives with measurable targets (raise $__, increase client base to ___, reduce costs by ___%), develop ways to achieve them (solicit donations from corporate sponsors, hold a fundraiser, install energy-saving light bulbs), and then break those down into individual actions that have assigned responsibility (development director writes fundraising letter, publications committee obtains quotes from printers, volunteer manager recruits 10 new docents).

There are many ways to structure plans. You may want to go online to compare common formats or ask other organizations what has worked best for them.

Most important, the plan should not be treated like the good silver, only to be brought out on holidays—it should be *used*. Knauss makes a point of saying that her organization's plan is more than a binder on a shelf. "This is very much a living, breathing, action-oriented, 'we're doing it' kind of plan."[10] Review the plan on a scheduled basis so that you can course-correct when tactics aren't working, the environment changes, funding sources don't pan out, new opportunities arise, or other unpredictable events occur.

CREATING A VOLUNTEER PROGRAM

"In their eagerness to reap the benefits of volunteer participation, organizational leadership may overlook the groundwork necessary to create and sustain a viable volunteer program."

—Jeffrey L. Brudney[11]

Dr. Brudney sums up the process of creating a volunteer program nicely: "To prepare the organization for volunteers, officials should set reasonable expectations concerning volunteers, establish an explicit rationale and goals for the volunteer program, involve paid staff in designing the program, implement a structural arrangement for housing the program and integrating it into the organization, create positions of leadership for the program, develop position descriptions for the tasks to be performed by volunteers, and design systems and supports to facilitate citizen participation and volunteer program management."[12]

Developing a volunteer program, then, requires far more than just bringing in people who have time to spare. It requires planning, preparation, organization, and the infrastructure necessary to ensure the program's long-term success.

Many volunteer programs make the mistake Maureen Eccleston, Director of Volunteer Maryland, calls "putting all their eggs in the recruitment basket." "The biggest misconception [about running a successful volunteer group] is that people think it's all about recruitment and they miss the other pieces that are necessary to have a solid volunteer program," says Eccleston. "People tend to focus on having nice recruitment materials, having a great recruitment campaign, and all of that's important, but they may miss the other elements that enable that volunteer to stay."[13] This means making a commitment to developing sound policies and procedures, building effective training programs, creating appealing volunteer opportunities and matching the right volunteers to them, recognizing and rewarding volunteers, and developing ways to evaluate and measure the effectiveness of the volunteer program.

Looking at the volunteer program in a holistic way also means treating volunteers as strategic assets to the organization—people who can potentially contribute on many levels. This includes bringing people into the organization that are willing and able to become real partners in furthering the organization's mission.

David Eisner and colleagues offered this example in an article on "the new volunteer workforce": Jim had 13 years with General Electric Co. and 28 years at J. P. Morgan when he volunteered to help the March of Dimes Foundation with strategic planning, marketing, information technology, training, and research. His wife, Sari, became a volunteer as well, and helped recruit 42 volunteers who donated a total of more than 11,000 hours. Jim and Sari became financial donors, and their daughter and son also became volunteers.[14] Jim (and his family) became a vital part of the organization, contributing on many levels. He was more than a volunteer—he was a strategic asset.

The authors argue that by finding ways to fully appreciate volunteers' skills and talents, organizations can not only see immediate benefits, but also will be more likely to retain the volunteers. They propose a "talent management approach" that requires investing in the infrastructure to recruit, develop, place, recognize, and retain volunteer talent.[15] "By treating volunteers as the valuable resource they are, nonprofits get more challenging work done, reap the benefit of more volunteer hours, and incur fewer costs associated with having to replace lost volunteers each year."[16]

Taking a strategic approach to recruitment is an essential part of developing a successful volunteer program. Ellis says, "The truth is that a lot of organizations are so grateful to have any volunteers, they think that having volunteers is the goal, and I say, that's ridiculous. What I want to know is, strategically, what are you saying the organization's mission is, and then—this year—what is it you're trying to accomplish, what have you set out for your goals. And then comes the question that I don't understand why more people don't ask, which is having just said what our organization's goals are for this year, how will volunteers—the right volunteers, not just warm bodies—help us to move forward on those goals. That's being strategic."[17]

BUDGETING

Budgeting puts a dollar number on the cost to implement a program or achieve a strategic goal. In this way you can decide which programs may not be feasible and which are good uses for the funds you have. You can also identify any projects that might be the object of a fundraising campaign or a grant application.

Here are some categories of expenses you will want to include in the budget to support volunteers, depending upon what is covered by other parts of the organization's budget (you will itemize within these categories):

- Facility costs
- Equipment, services, and supplies (computer, phone, Internet access, office supplies, photocopies, postage, etc.)
- Salaries (if applicable)
- Recruiting
- Training (manual, handouts, speaker costs, other materials)
- Volunteer materials (name badges, uniforms/aprons/tee shirts and gear, recognition and awards)

- Activity or program costs (itemized by activity or program)
- Advertising and promotion
- Website/social media
- Event/fundraiser costs
- Insurance
- Legal and other professional services (grant proposal writing, for example)

You will also want to budget revenues (sources of income such as grants and other funding sources, events/fundraisers, donations, training fees, etc.). Having a budget gives you a way to control costs, but it also provides a way to allocate by choice rather than by happenstance.

INHERITING A VOLUNTEER PROGRAM

If you are a newly hired manager, you will want to assess the current situation before deciding what, if any, changes you want to make to the volunteer program. Begin by examining the "bones"—the underlying structure or foundation. You may want to start by answering these questions:

- How many volunteers are there and how long have they been with the program?
- Are there enough volunteers to successfully accomplish the goals?
- Have the volunteers been fully trained?
- Are volunteers being scheduled and used effectively?
- Are well-written policies, procedures, and guidelines in place?
- Have there been any serious problems or concerns that remain unresolved (financial mismanagement, political infighting, accusations of abuse or harassment, lawsuits or insurance issues, facility or equipment problems, issues with reputation or image)?
- Are the volunteers happy with their assignments and with the organization?
- Is the volunteer program funded, or is there an immediate need to obtain revenues?
- Are volunteers working cooperatively with each other and with paid staff?
- How is the volunteer program viewed by the paid staff and board?
- How satisfied are constituents with the quality, availability, and variety of services provided by the organization?

- What projects or activities have been done in the past and how success-ful were they?
- What projects or activities are currently underway?
- Are records being kept properly and data being compiled in a way that facilitates evaluation and documentation?

The answers to some of these questions may be obvious or easily obtained through observation and a little research. For others, you may want to survey the volunteers, the paid staff, and possibly the constituents.

Surveys generally provide quantitative (numerical) information that is easy to compile and analyze, while interviews and focus groups are best for qualitative (opinion-based) information and idea generation. People tend to share more when they are given the opportunity to talk but may not be as honest, particularly if they feel they need to impress or please the person conducting the interview. Online surveys can be evaluated more objectively but do not allow you to ask for clarification and are less suited for open-ended questions such as "Have you found your volunteer work rewarding?"

You may also want to try roundtable discussions. These should be struc-tured to encourage brainstorming and idea exchange. You should commu-nicate that you are seeking input for cooperatively addressing the problems and developing practical solutions (not just continuing to com-plain about the problems). Include a way to record what is contributed and then get back to the participants with a summary of the ideas, includ-ing which ones you are acting on and why, and which ideas cannot be implemented, and why not.

You may want to include members of the paid staff and board in these discussions as well. Concentrate first on how well the organization's mis-sion is being furthered and how well the infrastructure (policies, proce-dures, training program, organization, and reporting structure) supports the volunteers, serves the organization and its constituents, and allows for growth.

STAFF VERSUS VOLUNTEER TASKS

"Noah's Ark was built by volunteers; the Titanic was built by paid staff."

As part of the planning process, you will work with members of the paid staff to determine which activities could involve volunteers, what kinds of volunteers are needed, who will train and supervise the volunteers, and how volunteer tasks will mesh with tasks performed by paid staff. You will also need to identify any additional skills that are needed and whether volunteers could supply them.

One mistake managers sometimes make is bringing in volunteers that are just like the paid staff. Susan Ellis says, "It's a mistake for a couple of reasons; first, it can set up tension with the paid staff, because now you do have a degree of who's doing what and why. But most importantly, instead of expanding the variety of what's available to help clients, you're keeping everybody homogenous and that's a misuse of the potential of the volunteers."[18]

Another mistake is assuming volunteers are unskilled and so assigning them easy but uninspiring work: sweeping floors, entering data, making fundraising calls, and so forth. By "dumbing down" tasks for volunteers, you do a disservice to both the volunteer and the organization.

Volunteers may well have valuable skills and may also be looking for ways to use them, especially if they are not using them at work. To determine whether people ever volunteer to satisfy needs not being met by a paid job, researchers studied volunteers at three social service organizations. They found that some people are indeed looking for more challenging work when they volunteer.[19] This suggests that there are a significant number of volunteers looking for assignments with some complexity.

Unfortunately, these kinds of skills go unused by volunteer programs when volunteers are corralled into one-size-fits-all positions and not given options. A study by the Corporation for National and Community Service found that most volunteers do not perform service activities that relate to their professional or occupational skills. Many volunteers engage in fundraising, which though very important, takes them away from opportunities to use their skills in other, possibly more valuable, ways. The study also found that volunteers who use their skills appear to be more likely to continue serving the organization year to year.[20] A 2003 survey of volunteer management capacity among charities and congregations conducted by the Urban Institute found that charities benefit from giving volunteers a variety of options to contribute to the operations of the organization, ranging from direct service to bookkeeping to advocacy and fundraising.[21]

This may explain why some organizations have difficulty obtaining and holding on to volunteers. Ellis says, "The people having recruiting problems are the organizations that have one thing for someone to do and that's it, so it's either yes or no ... but more importantly, it's the people who don't want input—they want to define all the work that's done, in other words, they treat volunteers as a cheap temp agency. And for the most part, that's not what people are looking for ... they want to feel that their efforts are making a difference in some way. It doesn't mean that they have to feel that they're creating world peace. But I think that too many organizations are still basically sharing low-level assignments and are not focused on the things people want to do."[22]

If there are less pleasant tasks that must be done, try to combine them with more appealing ones in natural groupings to make a unified volunteer position that not only makes sense, but also provides a stimulating experience for the volunteer. While you may have volunteers who are brain surgeons by day and thus enjoy a brainless activity like stuffing envelopes at night, you may also have lawyers who are willing to provide legal advice, teachers who would be great working with children or training other volunteers, and artists or writers who can help with brochures and newsletters.

Just because a particular task has historically been done by volunteers, don't assume that is the best way to accomplish that task. Some considerations that should go into differentiating which tasks should be assigned to volunteers and which to staff include:

- Insurance, risk, and liability issues
- Skills and capabilities of the paid staff
- Skills and capabilities of the volunteers
- The cost of outsourcing the task to an outside company or organization
- The importance of the task to the health of the organization
- The time required to complete the task
- The potential to break the task down into smaller components
- Whether having a volunteer perform the task has a greater impact for the client, the organization, or the community

Try to provide a hierarchy of tasks to offer some upward mobility. This will allow you to continue to challenge and provide rewards for volunteers who stick with the program. The hierarchy can be as simple as creating distinctions such as trainee, apprentice, junior volunteer, and senior volunteer. You can also make higher positions such as team leader and committee head dependent on attaining longevity or skill levels.

Deciding which tasks to assign to volunteers, then, should involve two viewpoints:

1. The skills, abilities, availability, and willingness of the volunteers
2. The skills, abilities, availability, and cost of the paid staff

You also have to consider any personnel policies and legal or insurance requirements that specify what paid staff (or volunteers) may or may not do. For example, in some groups, only paid staff can handle money.

Consider volunteers for these kinds of activities:

- Tasks that require little or no special training or skills
- Tasks that require specific skills (for which you can recruit volunteers with those skills)
- Tasks that can be performed by two or more people (and therefore might be appropriate for volunteer teams)
- Projects that advance the mission and that could be undertaken if a volunteer workforce were assembled
- Projects whose value would be greatly increased through volunteer involvement (a fundraiser, for example)
- Tasks that can be performed at any time, at a volunteer's convenience
- Tasks that do not have to be performed on site
- Tasks that are limited in scope (individual projects)
- Tasks that have little or no legal/insurance liability or other risk exposure
- Tasks that require little, if any, direct supervision
- Tasks that are not time dependent or that don't have tight deadlines
- Tasks that have a broad acceptable standard (no one "right" way, so they allow for different approaches)
- Tasks that expand the reach of the organization or the breadth of its services

Ideally, there is a good mesh between paid staff and volunteers. This will encourage sharing of responsibility in resource-maximizing ways. If, for example, you find a volunteer who has experience writing grant proposals (lucky you), the staff member responsible for fundraising may be able to spend more time cultivating individual donors while the volunteer takes on some of the grant proposal writing responsibility.

Organizations are increasingly reevaluating which tasks should be performed by volunteers rather than paid staff. More and more, volunteers are considered a vital part of the organization, working alongside the paid staff to advance the organization's goal. By thinking creatively, you may find new ways to structure projects and activities so that volunteers can participate in more significant ways than in the past.

QUESTIONS TO GET YOU STARTED

1. What are three goals you would like to reach within three years?
2. For each of those goals, what would be an achievable milestone for this year?
3. For each of those milestones, what resources will you need (volunteers, funding, staff support) in order to reach it?
4. In what ways could you be more strategic in your approach to recruiting, training, placing, recognizing, and retaining volunteers?

CHAPTER 2

Recruiting Good Volunteers

> The best way to find yourself is to lose yourself in the service of others.
>
> —Mahatma Gandhi[1]

WHY DO PEOPLE VOLUNTEER?

Social scientists have studied why people volunteer and identified a wide range of reasons. For example, a 1987 Canadian study suggested these three categories of volunteer motivation: self-interest, obligation, and altruism.[2] Common self-interest motives include wanting to learn, meet people, network, and prepare for a paying job. Obligation motives include required community service, church projects, and activities relating to race, culture, or community. Altruism motives are a desire to help others, contribute to a cause, or improve the world. Political activism falls into this category as well.

David McClelland (*Human Motivation*, 1985) focused on these three motives: the need for achievement, the need for affiliation, and the need for power. The need for achievement is an unconscious drive to do better toward a standard of excellence. People with tendencies toward this motivation like to measure their progress toward a goal. They set goals, take moderate risks, prefer individual activities, and enjoy activities that are scored or measured, especially when performance data are clearly available. The need for power is an unconscious drive to have impact on others. People with strong power motivation often take leadership positions, prefer competitive activities, and like to help or have impact on others. The need for affiliation is an unconscious drive to be a part of a relationship or group. People with strong affiliation motivation prefer to work in groups, are sensitive to others' reactions, enjoy collaborative activities, and like activities in which they work closely with others.[3]

No matter how you classify motivation, for most volunteers it is a mixture of motives, often from more than one category. Common reasons people give for volunteering are:

- Feeling a sense of accomplishment/reward
- Doing good deeds/serving others/achieving a goal
- Learning new skills
- Having the opportunity to use skills they already have
- Meeting new people/working with friends
- Working in a different environment or in a different way from their profession
- Gaining experience that will lead to paid work
- Using spare time productively

It is important to understand the reasons people volunteer not only to help you recruit volunteers, but also to help you manage them. As Maureen Eccleston explains, "If you know your volunteers well, if you know what their individual motivation is for wanting to volunteer, then that helps you to manage them better."[4] She says that knowing your volunteers is essential to placing them in the right positions—positions in which they will do a good job, be happy, and be inclined to stay with the organization.

Volunteer work is not as constrained as paid work. Most volunteers feel they have more autonomy (and less to fear) when working without pay. Volunteers are working because they want to, not because they have to, so in some ways they can be easier to motivate and be better workers (they are working for reasons other than just making a buck). So while it seems that you have fewer motivational arrows in your quiver, nonmonetary motivation can be stronger and more effective, particularly for the very people who volunteer in the first place. In addition, the goals they are working toward may be much more appealing to them (feeding the hungry as opposed to feeding the bottom line).

Motivations may change once the volunteer is on board. Someone who joined a volunteer program to meet people or improve job prospects may be inspired by the mission of the group. Another person might have joined because the organization's goals were appealing, only to find tremendous enjoyment working with like-minded people and learning new skills. Volunteers may also have an internal change in motives. They may, for example, develop a greater need for power. This is where the alert volunteer manager can provide stepping stones (committee chair, event manager, advisory board, etc.) to allow that volunteer to continue to have his or her motivations satisfied.

Knowing what motivates volunteers helps you tailor your task assignments and rewards. For example, a volunteer who is motivated by power will seek tasks that have significant impact or over which they will have control. Rewards might include increased visibility or a leadership role within the organization. A volunteer motivated by affiliation may be more interested in working as part of a team and in situations with a social component. These volunteers may appreciate volunteer appreciation events or branded items such as special nametags or shirts.

It is essential for the person who manages the volunteers to recognize individual differences in motivation and to provide volunteers with satisfactory experiences that meet their motivational needs and that evolve as the volunteer becomes a part of the group. For example, Jim Starr, Vice President of Volunteer Management for the American Red Cross, understands that as Red Cross volunteers become more involved with the group, they want to feel like they are a vital part of the organization. "Those that have been with us for a while . . . want to have the same level of insight and understanding of how we do things as an employee would. So when we make changes to our operational structure, or other kinds of things, or the things we support, they want to have that same level of input, feedback, and commitment to how we're doing things. It is critically important to make sure that you capture the voice of the volunteer in the things that you're doing as an organization."[5]

KINDS OF VOLUNTEERS

Some volunteer programs need long-term volunteers. Long-term volunteers stay with the group for a period of months or years, either performing the same duties during that time (such as someone who serves as a museum docent), a variety of duties (such as a volunteer at an animal shelter who walks dogs, cleans cages, and helps with adoption paperwork), or a sequence of projects (a volunteer who helps with a fundraiser and then prepares a museum exhibit). Other programs use short-term volunteers for tasks that last from a few hours to a few weeks. Most programs rely on a combination of both.

Many long-term volunteers have a strong emotional or philosophical attachment to the organization and its mission. These are volunteers who are dedicated to the work they do and consider themselves a part of the organization. Other long-term volunteers may have found a role they enjoy or people they like working with, or they may have just settled into a groove that works for them. Often (but not always) long-term volunteers are retirees, or other people without full-time paid jobs, who have large blocks of time and can make long-term commitments.

Short-term volunteers often have a general interest in the organization, a desire to help, and flexible schedules but may not want to (or can't) make a long-term commitment. These volunteers are often easier to find but may be harder to retain, although some volunteers simply prefer many short-term assignments to one long-term assignment. Short-term volunteers can become long-term volunteers, and in fact, a short-term assignment can be a trial period for both the volunteer and the organization.

Reasons for volunteering are varied for numerous reasons. A study on volunteers in Canada found the following:

- Volunteering changes throughout our life cycle, along with evolving priorities, circumstances, and interests.
- Today's volunteers are more goal-oriented, autonomous, tech-savvy, and mobile.
- Volunteering is a two-way relationship that needs to meet the goals of the volunteer and the organization.
- Volunteering is personal and stems from individual preferences and motivations.
- Volunteering is a way to transfer and develop skills by gaining or sharing experiences.
- Volunteering in groups appeals to all ages for social and business networking.
- Finding satisfying volunteering is not easy for everyone.[6]

ATTRIBUTES OF GOOD VOLUNTEERS

"Don't tell people how to do things, tell them what to do and let them surprise you with their results."

—George S. Patton[7]

Although the skills and abilities you look for in an applicant will vary by position, the type of program you have, the goals of the organization, and other factors, these are some characteristics you will tend to find in your best volunteers:

- *Reliability*. Without this, you have nothing. No matter how good their skills, how positive their attitudes, how willing they are to take charge and get the job done, if you cannot rely on volunteers to be where they say they will be, when they say they will be there, doing what they promised to do, they will create problems for you and the organization.
- *Flexibility*. What a great trait in a volunteer. "Can you work Monday instead of Tuesday?" Sure! "Would you mind stopping at the post office on your way home?" Not at all! "Could you be a greeter today instead of a cashier?" Absolutely!
- *Can-do attitude*. This means the difference between having to give every single direction and being able to do other things while a volunteer handles a project or activity. This is also the volunteer who will step up when needed and say, "I'll take care of that."
- *Multiple skills/abilities*. This is a huge bonus, particularly for small volunteer groups. Look for volunteers who have talents, skills, and experiences in a variety of areas. Pay particular attention to indications that a potential volunteer might be interested and able to become involved at multiple levels in the organization (as a volunteer *and* as a donor, for example).
- *Loyalty*. If you get an application that lists dozens of volunteer positions, each lasting no more than a few months, you should know what you are getting. If you are recruiting for a single project or event, it may not matter, but if you are investing time and money to train a volunteer, make sure the volunteer is committed to the program for a reasonable period of time.
- *Enthusiasm*. Don't underestimate this trait. Enthusiasm is the fuel that runs volunteer workforces. Enthusiasm is contagious, and it will rub off not only on other volunteers, but also on your constituents. I once hired (for a for-profit company) a woman who had been out of the workforce for a number of years. It was a risk, but her enthusiasm was phenomenal. She *really* wanted the job. It was one of the best hires I ever made.

ETHNIC AND CULTURAL DIVERSITY

It's fine to say you support equal opportunity and inclusivity, but in today's world, achieving diversity takes some effort.

Start by being welcoming. This means everything from making sure that the paid staff and existing volunteers are friendly and inclusive (offer sensitivity training if necessary) to making your events and activities as accessible as possible. Make sure you specifically state your commitment to diversity during volunteer training and tell volunteers you expect them to work with people from different backgrounds and cultures. Be alert for practices that make assumptions about people's religion, ethnicity, or other factors (holding a Christmas party, for example).

If your goal is to recruit minorities, don't overlook the power of asking. According to a report by Independent Sector, of all adults surveyed, people of color—specifically African Americans and Hispanics—were not asked to volunteer as frequently as their white counterparts. Yet when African Americans and Hispanics were asked to volunteer, they were just as likely to do so as other racial groups.[8]

Go where the volunteers you want live. If you want Spanish-speaking volunteers, recruit in Hispanic communities, preferably with the help of a Spanish-speaking volunteer. If you want a better racial balance, recruit in communities where the volunteers you want to attract live. Public libraries, community centers, and houses of worship are some of the locations where you might hold information sessions.

Keep in mind that a close-knit community may distrust outsiders. Enlisting the aid of a community leader can be a huge advantage. Having someone from the community talk about your organization at a comfortable location within the community is much more likely to produce interested applicants than a talk by someone they don't know at a place they are unfamiliar with.

Make sure your recruiting materials are specific to the position, not the person. Any requirements should be for tasks that cannot be modified. For example, if lifting heavy boxes is a necessary part of the position, it should be stated in the position description. However, if adaptations can be made (a riser to accommodate someone of short stature, for example), there is no need to state a height requirement. If social media skills are required, state specifically what skills are needed rather than assume you need a young person.

Eliminate sexism by avoiding the use of male pronouns and not making assumptions about gender when structuring or describing volunteer positions. You may lose a capable female applicant for a facilities position by using the title "handyman" or using "he" throughout the position description. Likewise, an office manager/secretary position should not be made available only to female applicants. State the requirements for the position in neutral terms ("must be able to lift 50 pounds," "must know how to prepare simple meals," "must have commercial driver's license") rather than presuming the kind of person that is likely to fit the bill.

Make sure your public face reflects diversity. If your website has photos only of young white women (as an example), you are likely to attract young white women. You don't need to make the site look like a United Nations meeting, but if you have some diversity in your group, make sure that it's reflected in the photos you choose.

If you hold meetings and events, be flexible so that you can involve as many people as possible. When you schedule meetings (especially anywhere you plan to recruit volunteers), consider holding them at times when people who work traditional business hours can attend. Hold meetings and events in locations near where the people you want to attract live or can easily get to (on a public transportation route, for example).

Watch for opportunities to offer tasks that can be performed by people with limited intellectual capability, reduced mobility, sight or hearing impairments, or other special issues. Some of the very tasks that many volunteers don't enjoy may be welcomed by volunteers who are not able to participate in other ways. An organization I worked with had a volunteer who had suffered a stroke that limited her ability to walk and participate in many activities, but she was delighted to have the opportunity to fold brochures, a task that did not interest other volunteers.

Be alert to the need to provide assistance, even if people have not specifically requested it. If you have volunteers with hearing impairments (as is common among older volunteers), you should use a microphone at all meetings and events. Using facilities that are accessible by elevators or ramps helps not only people in wheelchairs, but also older people with dodgy knees.

Make sure cost is not a barrier for volunteers. If there are charges associated with your volunteer program (a training component, for example), offer scholarships. If possible, offer to reimburse approved expenses, including mileage. Be sensitive to child care needs. If you have several volunteers who have young children, it may be worth having a volunteer (who has been properly screened and trained) provide onsite babysitting. If you are dealing with a disadvantaged population, you may want to provide nutritious food at the meeting.

Keep in mind that cultural and age differences can create awkward situations. If you are recruiting in a particular demographic, make sure you learn a little about it first. My mother's hairdresser learned that older people often appreciate a little more formality. She had asked my mother's name. My mother responded, "Day." The hairdresser said, "No, I meant your first name." My mother replied, "Mrs."

If your volunteers are primarily women (or men), older people (or younger), working people (or nonworking), a particular racial or cultural group, or any other demographic, think about ways of broadening your reach. Diversity of volunteers translates to diversity of ideas, capabilities, and talents. A diverse volunteer workforce will also help you reach a diverse audience. The result is a healthier and more effective volunteer program.

SKILL AND ROLE DIVERSITY

If you were a baseball manager, would you recruit nine shortstops? No. Would a football coach want only players who can throw long passes? Would a hockey team succeed with just goalies? Sports recruiters understand the need to fill the bench with players who have specialized skills that, when put together, make up a great team. Why then, do many volunteer managers ignore the need to round out their bench?

Some people are naturally leaders, and others are naturally followers. Most serve in a variety of roles (some as leaders and some as followers). When you recruit, try to get a sense of the role the potential volunteer wants and is able to play. You do not want all leaders or all followers. A good balance, depending on your needs, is to shoot for about 10 to 15 percent leaders. This will allow you to have project teams and committees of eight to 10 people under each leader.

You may also want to look for volunteers who could serve as advisors or mentors. These are volunteers who have either work or life experience that provides wisdom useful to the program. These kinds of people make great board members, or can serve on a steering committee to help advise you on decisions involving the volunteer program.

Look for skill diversity as well. For example, a team of volunteers working to create an exhibit for a historical society museum might include someone with good organizational skills, someone with a strong knowledge of local history, a graphic artist who can help create displays, and someone with a strong back to lift and move boxes. This sort of team would also make it possible to use the skills of someone with a mental or physical disability.

Skill and role diversity is particularly important in a board of directors. One approach is to consider "the three W's": wealth, wisdom, and work. Each board member should provide at least one of these attributes to your organization, and your board should contain a balance of these components.

RECRUITING FROM WITHIN THE ORGANIZATION

One of the best places to find volunteers is within your organization. Donors, family members of volunteers, members, and even clients or constituents may be willing to help out in a volunteer capacity. These are people who support the group's mission and activities, and they already know a little bit about how things are done, making the orientation process simpler.

Organizations that have a membership program can approach their members about volunteering, starting with a checkbox on the membership form that says: "I may be interested in volunteer opportunities." Some organizations include an interests checklist. This is a nonthreatening way to identify people who might respond to a specific request. For example, a project to create a mosaic wall for a building might be an opportunity to invite anyone who likes arts and crafts projects. You might even make a volunteer interests database that can be sorted and include when the volunteers are available (day, evening, weekend), any limitations (cannot lift heavy objects), and special skills (knows how to operate a tiller). Don't forget to include requests for specific types of volunteers in your newsletter or email communications to people within the organization.

You may also be able to approach people your group has touched. This works especially well for hospitals, support groups, schools, and social service organizations. Whenever an individual has received services or completed a term of use (graduated or otherwise moved on), a follow-up letter should be sent that includes a mention that volunteers are needed to help continue this good work. You can also post signs or posters in public areas such as waiting rooms or visiting areas. Personal calls can also be very effective ("I'm calling to congratulate you on your graduation and to ask whether you'd like to stay involved with our school").

Fundraisers and other special events are an excellent time to approach potential volunteers. Make a point of greeting any unfamiliar guests. After introductions, simply asking "Are you familiar with the work our group is doing?" can start a conversation that enables you to mention the need for volunteers. Keep these conversations short (you don't want to interfere with the person's enjoyment of the event) but try to get the person's contact information so that you can follow up the next day with an "it was a pleasure meeting you" email that outlines your volunteer needs. Ideally, you will have made notes so that you can be specific. ("Based on what you told me about your background, you would be a great help to us with _____.") Even if you don't get a new volunteer, perhaps the person will become a member or agree to receive your newsletter, increasing the odds for future volunteering. If the person was at all receptive, create a reminder to send an email in six months to see if his or her situation has changed.

Your most important tool in this kind of recruiting may be simple observation. Notice people that are appearing at your events and functions. One reason people donate time (and money) is to feel important. Acknowledging involvement lets people know you respect them and value their contributions.

Recognizing supporters also helps them step from one role (occasional support) to the next (loyal support or perhaps direct involvement through donation or volunteerism). Here's an example: My husband and I attended a few shows at a local theater. Then we became members at the basic level. The following year, we bought season tickets. I frequently posted positive comments on their Facebook page. We even attended a fundraiser. Could I have provided any more signals indicating my support? Why, then, did no one contact me to say, "Hey, we noticed you are supporting us! Would you consider becoming a volunteer?" I wouldn't have volunteered on my own, but with that kind of invitation, it would be pretty hard to resist! Who doesn't like to be noticed?

Along these lines, make sure you have a solid inquiry response system in place. I had to send three emails in response to one organization's request for volunteers before someone answered me. Another prospective volunteer may not have tried as hard. Treat volunteer inquiries like money—too valuable to be misplaced or allowed to drop between the sofa cushions.

One of the primary ways people start volunteering is by someone they know asking them. In the survey "Giving and Volunteering in the United States," more than four out of ten (45 percent) of the volunteers said they learned about a volunteer activity from someone they know, most often by a friend (52 percent), someone at their religious congregation (38 percent), or by a family member or relative (30 percent).[9]

People enjoy working with friends (something that is seldom possible in the world of paid work), so asking your volunteers to invite their friends to join them is likely not only to add new volunteers to your program, but also to increase the satisfaction of the volunteers you have. Consider a "bring a friend" event, at which existing volunteers can introduce friends to the group. Ask your volunteers to promote your volunteer openings on their Facebook pages or other friend networks and specifically ask volunteers if they know anyone who might be a good addition to the program.

Friends of volunteers may also be easier to retain. A study conducted by the Urban Institute found that volunteers recruited one-on-one by existing volunteers had higher retention rates than those recruited through other means. The authors said: "Enlisting volunteers as 'spokespersons' for the charity in this manner implies a level of trust in these participants, evidence of both a supportive organizational culture and confidence that the charity provides a worthwhile experience to volunteers."[10]

Don't overlook family members. Invite the spouses or partners, parents, and children (where appropriate) of existing volunteers to join your efforts. Provide opportunities for families to work on volunteer projects together. If your group serves children, consider their parents as potential volunteers.

Lynn Spreadbury says Save the Children makes a major effort to keep volunteers involved in the organization and finds that volunteers are one of their best recruiting tools when they return home from remote assignments. "We try to think of them as being ambassadors for the organization when they go back," she says.[11]

RECRUITING PAST VOLUNTEERS

There's a principle in marketing that says it is easier to get business from an old customer than to convince someone who has never tried your product to give it a try. For this reason, past volunteers are also potential new recruits.

A study conducted in Canada found that 33 percent of Canadians were not currently volunteering but had done so in the past. The study's results also shed light on the barriers, challenges, and disappointments the volunteers encountered that resulted in their leaving the organization. This led the authors to theorize that the most promising opportunity for expanding the volunteer base is to recruit past volunteers. This can be done by addressing their issues—such as perceived organizational politics or not feeling that they were making a real difference—and by helping match their interests and skills with activities that will have a direct benefit. Almost a third (31 percent) of past volunteers said they would likely volunteer in the next 12 months, and 76 percent indicated that they would recommend volunteering to others. Volunteers tend to be loyal even though some felt their expectations for the volunteer experience were not met to their satisfaction.[12]

Find out why a particular volunteer left your program. If job or family commitments were an issue, perhaps you can rearrange the schedule to suit their needs. If the volunteer didn't enjoy a particular task, talk about other tasks that are available. Was there a personality issue or organizational problem that has since been resolved? Maybe the volunteer felt unappreciated. Or it could be that the volunteer just wanted to take a break.

Think of ways to reach out to past volunteers. Jason Zigmont, founder of VolunteerFD.org, a web-based resource for volunteer firefighters, suggests throwing an "old timers" party. He points out that schools throw reunions every five years. Why not hold volunteer reunions to get past volunteers fired up again?[13]

Look for ways to stay in touch with past volunteers. Maintain a database that includes past volunteers and (unless they don't want to receive it) send them the newsletter or other communications. The database should include tasks the volunteers have done, dates, and any other information you find helpful (such as special skills or in which facility they worked). You can use this information in several ways. If you have a particular position to fill, you can sort by skill or by the task they performed in the past. ("I see you helped at our event two years ago. We have a similar event coming up in the fall. Would you be willing to give us a hand?") You might also sort by date and set up a tickler file to contact people who haven't volunteered for a set period of time to see if you can encourage them to return. You could also sort by address if you have a position open in a particular geographic area.

RECRUITING FROM THE COMMUNITY

People like to volunteer close to home. Not only is it more convenient, but also working close to home means that the volunteers' efforts are directed at their own community. Ideally, you already have a presence in the community. If not, start to build visibility. You may wish to participate in fairs or parades, public service events (community cleanup days, for example), or career fairs.

Independent Sector's studies have shown that the more "linked" a person is to his or her community, the more likely it is that the person will volunteer. "People who are active in social networks in a local community give back to that community. Active participation in a social network can take the form of membership in a religious institution or participation in various civic or social clubs, sports clubs or hobby groups."[14]

Open houses and other on-site events are another way of attracting potential volunteers. It will help if you provide some educational or entertainment content to attract prospects. Possibilities include a guest speaker, a fair (activities for children, live music, etc.), free access to something you generally charge for, a celebrity appearance, or something else that will draw an audience.

Public information sessions or talks on subjects related to your mission are excellent ways to promote your group and publicize your need for volunteers. Public libraries often allow their facilities to be used for educational talks. If you use youth volunteers, you may want to seek out a school club, after-school program, or scouting group. If you have an appropriate space at your facility, you can hold talks there.

A wide variety of organizations use outside speakers for their own meetings. Likely candidates include civic or social clubs, business organizations, garden clubs, newcomer organizations, faith groups, parent/teacher groups, homeowner associations, women's groups, arts organizations, senior centers, community centers, advocacy organizations, and support groups. Look particularly for organizations with goals and interests that match yours. For example, Lions Clubs have historically been associated with collecting eyeglasses and might be very interested in hearing from an organization that is involved with the blind, a library that uses people to read books aloud, or a group that trains guide dogs. If you have a volunteer who is a member of the organization you are speaking to, see if that person will accompany you.

The best approach is an educational presentation on a topic of general interest, rather than a self-promotional talk about your organization. For example, an animal shelter might offer a talk on how to choose a new pet. A volunteer fire company might offer a talk about emergency preparedness. You can mention the need for volunteers at the end of the talk and emphasize how important they are to your organization. In that way, the talks serve a double purpose: educating the public and getting the word out that you are looking for volunteers.

The person giving the talk should be enthusiastic and be able to convey that the volunteers enjoy themselves. Use attractive visuals whenever possible, and consider bringing "eye candy" connected with your constituents—art projects children made, thank you notes from grateful medical care recipients, a flower arrangement created by seniors, and so on.

A particularly effective speaker is someone from the constituency you reach. For example, a school might have a former student speak about how the experience changed his or her life. A food bank might have someone who was helped through a difficult period. These kinds of personal narratives can be very powerful and persuasive.

If your organization holds an annual fund drive or membership/donor appeal, consider taking advantage of the visibility those kinds of activities create. Even a one-time event such as a building fund drive can provide a vehicle for you to reach potential volunteers.

You don't want to take advantage in a tasteless way, but if you can use a current news story to generate interest in helping your cause, it can be a powerful motivator to potential volunteers. Examples include natural disasters (even if they are not in your area), stories of abused or neglected animals, new statistics on health conditions or people in need, stories about reduced funding for the arts, or environmental problems.

You can also piggyback on national events or theme dates. For example, you might time your appeal with a nationwide volunteer event such as National Volunteer Week. The anniversary of a key event (your organization's founding or other milestone, a well-known national event or historical date) can be another kind of tie-in.

Networking in the community can also be a way to find volunteers. Join local organizations, local chapters of national organizations, and attend job fairs, business card exchanges, and other networking events. This can be a particularly good way to meet people with specialized skills (legal, medical, business) who might provide professional services as volunteers.

See if there are any volunteer fairs in your area. These are great opportunities to recruit people who are already interested in volunteering and are just looking for a good match for their interests and skills. You might also consider a booth at a community event, senior expo, health fair, or farmers market. These are all opportunities to inexpensively interact with the public and communicate your need for volunteers. Wherever you go, be sure to have plenty of literature and volunteer applications!

TARGETED RECRUITING

> Simply asking is one of the most effective ways to get people involved. When asked to volunteer, over 85 percent will say yes!
>
> —Nadine Jalandoni and Keith Hume[15]

It is always easier to fish in a stocked pond. I once had a friend who joined a Corvette club. I asked her why (she didn't own a Corvette), and she told me that she wanted to meet men who owned Corvettes. I'm not sure I approve of this technique for finding a husband, but it is a good approach for finding volunteers.

Go to the places where the kinds of people you want to recruit are likely to be found. If your group has to do with animal care, post notices at veterinarian offices, dog parks, kennels, and animal day care centers. If your group has to do with medicine, distribute information at health fairs, and post notices on hospital and medical office bulletin boards and on websites for support groups. Think about where the kinds of people you want as volunteers might be found—that is where you want to be with your recruiting message.

Targeted recruiting also has the benefit of helping you to find volunteers with specific skills, from particular backgrounds (for diversity), or from specific geographic areas. If you know you need specific kinds of volunteers, recruit in a target-rich environment. Do you need people with public speaking skills? Make a presentation to a local Toastmasters meeting or seek out professors or clergy members. Need help with social media? Put a sign in a computer store or place an ad in a school newspaper.

For some volunteer assignments, you are better off determining the person you want and then going after that specific individual. This may be the case for tasks needing professional skills (such as accounting or legal expertise), positions requiring specialized talents (managing large work teams or running an important event), and board or steering committee positions. For these kinds of volunteers, you may want to seek out (through personal referrals, recommendations, or networking) possible candidates and then approach those individuals to determine their interest and availability.

How you ask someone to volunteer can make all the difference. You can use the same tone and wording as when you ask a teenager to take out the trash (and get about the same amount of cooperation), or you can present the opportunity like a bouquet of roses.

Start by explaining why you chose this particular person. Praise the skills, experience, personality traits, and talents that make the person right for the position. Then explain why the group needs the person to do this task (the big picture—the need to increase revenues so that vital services won't be lost, not the need to have someone create a database for a fundraiser). Provide a fair description of what the work entails, including the time requirements. Be sure to include any favorable components (the work can be done from home, there is a generous deadline, the position has high visibility). When talking with the prospect, use the word "you," not "volunteer" or "someone." Keep it personal and targeted.

In the for-profit world, sales representatives are trained to ask for the sale. It's the most important question, but the one that's most often missed. That's because many of us are shy when it comes to just asking for what we want, especially if we don't know the person well. Yet according to experts, "even highly motivated people are unlikely to volunteer unless they are asked, and people with little motivation to volunteer might agree to do so if they are constantly badgered by friends to give some of their time."[16] This is particularly true for older people. "Seniors were approximately five times more likely to volunteer if they were asked. Even people 75 years and older of age volunteered at a high rate when asked. Approximately 81% of seniors over 75 years of age volunteered when asked, compared to only 25% when they were not asked."[17]

RECRUITING TOOLS: PRINTED MATERIALS

Volunteer recruiting begins with making the organization visible, appealing, and motivating. Make people want to be part of your team. When you create materials for public audiences, avoid insider jargon, acronyms, and abbreviations that are not explained. It makes people feel left out, or even stupid, and makes the organization seem less approachable. Remember that some of the people reading your materials may not be fluent in your language. Keep words and sentences simple. This will also help boost your diversity. People who have trouble deciphering your position description and volunteer information will not feel welcome and, as a result, may not apply.

If you have a general brochure, it should have a section on volunteering. This should include details about the kinds of volunteers you need, what the volunteers do, requirements (background checks or licenses needed), and benefits (to the volunteer) of volunteering.

Desktop publishing makes it easy to create brochures targeted to specific audiences. For this reason, you should consider creating a brochure specifically targeted to potential volunteers. You may even want to create different brochures for different audiences. The brochures should focus on the ways in which volunteers are used, the opportunities available to volunteers, and the importance of their work. Don't forget to include contact information and perhaps even a preliminary application form, so if readers are interested they can act on that interest immediately.

If you have a physical facility, you should consider a sign, free-standing display, bulletin board, or other vehicle that highlights volunteer activities, successes, and needs. You might include pictures of volunteers in action, award ceremonies, or appreciation events. Even this display should have a "call to action." Include something like "Want to join us? Call xxx-xxxx" or place a stack of volunteer brochures or applications next to the display.

Try to be as descriptive as you can. The words "Ask about volunteer opportunities" followed by a phone number will not get a great response. Most people will not step forward until they know a little about what they are getting into. Instead, create messages that convey your organization's mission or appeal to specific types of volunteers. Here are some examples:

- 20% of the children in our area go to bed hungry each night. Want to help change that?

- Enjoy teaching? We're looking for volunteers to teach seniors basic computer skills
- Help us take home-cooked meals to homebound parishioners
- Retired? Let us show you how you can make a difference in a child's life
- Do you have an hour a week to help us find homes for neglected animals?
- Good with numbers? We are looking for a volunteer bookkeeper

Mention any incentives you can offer volunteers. These might include memberships, tee shirts, gift shop discounts, free tickets, guest passes, and other items that are worth more than what they cost you. There may be other perks you can offer—VIP status or being put to the top of waiting lists, badges that provide extra privileges, special seating at events, and advance notice and the ability to purchase tickets before the general public. Don't forget intangible but valuable benefits such as getting to go behind the scenes, job training, networking opportunities, and access to celebrities or VIPs. If being part of your organization allows volunteers to help shape public policy or change community conditions, make that clear. These kinds of incentives are "pay" you can offer your volunteers.

RECRUITING TOOLS: PUBLICITY

If you don't already have press contacts, start to cultivate them. A friendly reporter at a local newspaper or television station can do wonders for your organization. Make reporters aware of your group by sending out press releases on a regular basis. In addition, make local reporters aware of your areas of expertise. That way, when the reporter is doing a story on a topic that relates to one of these areas, you may be called for an interview. Offer authority interviews, statistics, photographs, and other resources that make reporters' jobs easier. When you are interviewed, be sure to mention the vital role of volunteers.

Many papers have sections in which volunteer needs are posted. Be sure to take advantage of these. If your local paper does not have such a section, prepare a very short item that describes your need for volunteers and ask the paper to include it as a filler item whenever there is space. Look for online publications as well as print. Radio and television stations often allot time for public service announcements.

Look for opportunities for ongoing publicity (contributing to a blog, a weekly or monthly column in a newspaper, a periodic TV segment, etc.).

Think of a good hook that will appeal to the reporter as well as the public ("Adopt a Family for Christmas," "Scout of the Month," "Timely Gardening Reminders," "Food Bank Wish List," etc.). Any time you create anything for the press, be sure to mention the need for volunteers.

RECRUITING TOOLS: WEBSITES, ELECTRONIC COMMUNICATION, AND SOCIAL MEDIA

A good website is essential to volunteer recruitment efforts. Potential volunteers are likely to go to your site before making a commitment. Use your website to highlight your volunteer program and to communicate volunteer events, activities, and accomplishments. Keep information current, replace photos often, and add fresh information frequently. Be sure to mention specifics such as minimum age, any special skill or experience requirements, times volunteers are generally needed, any training required or provided, and so forth. Anticipate the questions a potential volunteer might ask, then answer them so that you don't have to waste time with phone calls or email from ineligible prospects.

Provide information on specific kinds of volunteers you need (office, docents, greeters, patient/pet interaction, food/event preparation, teaching/working with children, etc.). Include photographs (or even links to YouTube videos) of volunteers in action to give potential volunteers the opportunity to see what being a volunteer for the group is like. Always provide a link to request additional information and a telephone number that will be answered by someone knowledgeable about the volunteer program (not just the main office number). You may want to include an online application.

Provide opportunities for viral dissemination. Promote events by creating a badge or widget people can use on their own blogs or websites. Provide text, photos, and videos designed for sharing, and post compelling stories that visitors will be inclined to pass on. Consider creating real-time interactive activities such as webinars or online chats.

Volunteer position vacancies posted on the website are ideally more than just a position description. Although you will want to clearly describe the tasks required, also include a little about the kind of person best for the task and the nature of the position itself. Here are some examples: "this position is ideal for someone who likes to work from home in his or her spare time and is good with computer graphics," "a bright sunny personality is a great asset for this position, which includes greeting people as they enter our building," "this position can be a little tedious, but for someone who likes low-stress work that allows the mind to roam a bit, it is just the ticket," or "compassion is required for this position, which involves working with people who are grieving, but the reward is great, as you are playing a part in helping people through a very difficult point in their life."

Here are a few websites that do a particularly good job of conveying what their volunteers do:

United Nations Volunteers (http://www.unv.org)

Wings for Success (http://wingsforsuccess.org)

Boys and Girls Clubs (http://www.boysgirlsclubs.org/)

Social media can be a very effective (and nearly free) way for a volunteer program to gain visibility and recruit volunteers. Ideally, one or more volunteers will take on this assignment, as consistency is a key part of a successful social media presence.

An active, consistent, and engaging Facebook page is an excellent place to start. Your posts should reflect the purpose, activities, and personality of your organization and its volunteer program. This helps potential volunteers get a sense of not only what the organization is about, but also what it would be like to be a part of it. Make several people administrators of the page, provide them with guidelines on appropriate content, and then encourage them to post timely, interesting, and educational content. For example, a health advocacy group might post links to the latest research, statistics, or information on pending legislation. The more interesting, useful, and interactive the content you post, the more fans (and volunteers) you will attract and the more often people will repost your information. Create Facebook events and post links to website content. Invite participants to spread the word and ask them to share your posts with friends. Questions, quizzes, contests, and other interactive content will boost both visits to the page and the numbers of "likes" it gets.

Twitter works well for groups that want to provide a sense of immediacy or connect with volunteers quickly. For example, if your group sponsors a run, you might have someone assigned to send out tweets from the sidelines (or even have a runner who is willing to tweet along the way) to update people on the progress of the race. A political group might tweet new polling numbers, the location of a candidate's appearance, or the need for canvassers. Twitter can be used to promote events, provide updates on facility changes, give fundraising updates, and share results of volunteer efforts. Twitter also allows you to spread the word about volunteer opportunities, hear what people are saying about your organization, keep volunteers informed, and find out what other groups are doing. It can be used for on-the-spot recruiting for immediate, short-term projects.

Although it was created by a clever individual, not an official representative of the Bronx Zoo, the Twitter account @BronxZoosCobra attracted more than 200,000 followers by pretending to be a snake that escaped from the zoo.[18] Hilarious tweets such as "Is it just me or did Medusa have the best hairstyle EVER?" and "Enjoying a cupcake @magno liabakery. This is going straight to my hips. Oh, wait. I don't have hips. Yesss!" rapidly went viral.[19] For some organizations, an unorthodox approach such as this can raise visibility for your mission and inspire people to want to join your volunteer ranks.

Blogs are another way to convey the personality of your group and make it attractive to potential volunteers. Blogs work particularly well for political or activist organizations because they are, by nature, voices of opinion. But blogs can also be used in other ways. A summer intern might blog about her experiences and activities. A church member might blog about progress toward completing a building addition, a new garden, or a fundraising project. Blogs work especially well for outreach efforts, for example, an overseas mission or a health facility in Africa, because it gives potential volunteers a sense of the importance of the organization's efforts. A blog could also be used to make recommendations, give advice, or provide guidance, and of course a blog could profile volunteers and announce volunteer opportunities.

E-newsletters are another inexpensive and very easy way to keep potential volunteers aware of what the organization is doing and to recruit new volunteers. Sources such as Constant Contact and Vertical Response provide easy-to-use templates and allow you to upload email lists for people who have agreed to receive your newsletter.

Pinterest offers a way to provide visual content in a bulletin board format. This works well for groups such as historical societies, arts organizations, and libraries, which can develop boards that feature objects from their collections, recommended books, and so forth, for people to "repin," which spreads the word about their organizations. Pinterest boards can also be used to tell a story or provide a personality for the organization; they can be quirky, esoteric, emotional, artistic, or serious. A theater group might pin photos of costumes, scenery, or set decorations that are graphically appealing. An animal protection organization might pin pictures of adorable animals.

YouTube videos are another way to attract potential volunteers. How-to demonstrations, informational clips, videos from events, and behind-the-scenes tours are perfect ways to introduce not only potential volunteers but also potential members, donors, board members, and the general public to the organization.

One of the most significant trends in social media is localization. From apps that suggest restaurants based on your location to new social media that let you know when someone who shares your interests is nearby, these tools are providing ways for companies and organizations to target their prospects more finely (and cost effectively) than ever before. Smartphones have made it possible to target volunteer opportunities down to the individual level and allow volunteers to participate immediately. For example, VolunteerMatch has a smartphone app that allows potential volunteers to review and sign up for local assignments and then share those activities with their friends and family.

The flip side of this is that social media is also global. This allows you to potentially attract volunteers from anywhere in the world. Consider this when structuring volunteer opportunities, and try to identify tasks that can be performed from any location.

Online recruitment sites have made it easy for volunteer programs to reach out to individuals who are considering donating time. Sites such as Craigslist, LinkedIn, and Monster.com are mainstream vehicles, used by for-profit companies to recruit paid employees, but they also allow organizations to post volunteer positions. VolunteerMatch is a dedicated national nonprofit site that allows qualified nonprofit organizations to post volunteer openings.

On these sites, as in your other materials, you will be more successful if you take the time to think through both the volunteer opportunity and the way in which it is described. Here is an example of a position posted by StudentMentor.org:

> Impart your life-long learning and experience to mentor up-and-coming college students in your industry or field. As a mentor, you decide the length of the mentorship and have the flexibility of meeting virtually or in-person. Here is a brief list of benefits:
>
> • Enhance your leadership, management, and coaching skills
> • Experience both personal and professional growth
> • Support and foster the next generation by serving as a role model[20]

This is a very appealing post because it emphasizes the importance of the task, the flexibility of the position, and the benefits to the volunteer. VolunteerMatch also allows you to indicate whether the position is local or virtual, and to flag its suitability for "kids," "55+," "teens," and "groups." It is appropriate for one-time volunteer tasks, long-term positions, and board opportunities.

Instant messaging, Twitter, smartphones, and other new technologies and media are making it possible for organizations to take advantage of crowdsourcing. This is a collaborative process that starts out with a call (a tweet or other communication) that attracts a group of unrelated people to solve a problem or participate in an activity. Crowdsourcing offers a way to generate fast response, community-level action, which can be appropriate for certain kinds of organizations and activities.

By the time this book is published, there will undoubtedly be new online vehicles and forms of social media, as well as new ways to use them. Remember that social media is, well, *social*. Use the nature of the media to socialize with your public, and project an appealing, authentic, and inviting persona.

QUESTIONS TO GET YOU STARTED

1. What skills are you missing within the volunteer workforce that you would like to have?

2. Where are some places you might find the kinds of volunteers you want?

3. Are there some recruiting tools you haven't tried but that might be successful?

4. Who are some key people you might ask to volunteer?

5. Are you listing your volunteer opportunities on recruiting sites such as VolunteerMatch?

6. Can you identify any ways in which you might use social media for recruiting volunteers?

CHAPTER 3

Selection, Orientation, and Measurement

Three people were at work on a construction site. All were doing the same job, but when each was asked what the job was, the answers varied. "Breaking rocks," the first replied. "Earning my living," the second said. "Helping to build a cathedral," said the third.

—Peter Schultz[1]

THE POSITION DESCRIPTION

As with any job, paid or not, much aggravation can be spared by having a clear understanding of expectations upfront, and a good place to start is with a position description. The position description should describe any qualifications required and the tasks the volunteer will be asked to do. It should be vivid enough to excite and realistic enough to be honest. Try to paint a picture of what the position is like in a way that lets prospective volunteers put themselves into that setting and determine whether it would be a good fit. Ideally, the position description will convey to the volunteer not only the usefulness of the breaking of the rocks, but also their role in the building of a cathedral.

Try to structure any volunteer task or position so that the volunteer has some sense of "turf," or ownership. Most people perform better and have a greater sense of reward when they are taking care of something of their own. This is true even for smaller tasks. For example, rather than give volunteers a list of random numbers to call, carve out a geographic or demographic area that is "theirs" to cover (political groups actually call this cutting turf). Try to group tasks in logical ways and give different volunteers their own set of tasks to be responsible for. The grouping may be a project, a physical space, a group of constituents, or a content area. Make sure to allow volunteers to also take responsibility for planning, organizing, and evaluating the tasks as well. They will naturally want to do well and improve the results each time.

Choose the title and description of the position carefully. Avoid using the generic "volunteer" and instead create a title that has real meaning. Include the big picture—the meaningful part of the position—in addition to the details. It doesn't hurt to use a little marketing spin. Which sounds like more fun: Landscape Maintenance Worker or Park Tender? Employment Counselor or Job Coach? County Extension Horticulture Volunteer or Master Gardener? One animal shelter had trouble getting volunteers to go through lost animal data until they named the position Pet Detective.[2] Make the description appealing as well. Be honest, but use engaging language. For example, here are two different ways to name and describe the same position at a women's shelter:

Client Intake Worker
Conduct interviews, answer questions, assist with paperwork, and identify resources at a women's shelter.
Women's Advocate
Help women in crisis get support and encouragement by answering their questions while obtaining the information necessary to connect them with the services they need.

The first position sounds bureaucratic and boring; the second sounds important and interesting. The same position, presented differently.

A position description can also be used as an evaluation tool. To do that, you will need to include specific goals or evaluation criteria (e.g., see a certain number of patients, plant a specific number of trees, or serve a minimum number of hours).

In some cases, you may want to separate the goals from the description. For example, the position description may say that the volunteer will be responsible for calling area businesses to get donations for the annual fundraising auction. The volunteer's goals might be to bring in a minimum number of donations or donations of a specific dollar value. This way, you can change the goals each year, while the position description remains the same.

Here are the pieces of information typically included in a position description:

- Title
- General description of the position and how it contributes to the organization's mission
- Qualifications (including any tests, certifications, or licenses needed)
- Requirements (physical requirements, language ability, computer expertise, etc.)
- Supervision (who will monitor and evaluate the volunteer's work)
- Tasks to be performed
- Time commitment and schedule (number of hours per week, for example)
- Where the work will be performed
- What, if any, expenses will be reimbursed
- How the volunteer's work will be evaluated
- Training requirements (including who will provide it and who will pay for it)
- Items necessary (uniform, safety equipment, tools, vehicle, and whether the volunteer must supply them)
- Dress code or other regulations
- Any requirements for confidentiality, fiduciary responsibility, client privacy
- Any required recordkeeping
- Benefits to the volunteer (tangible perks such as discounts and subscriptions, as well as intangibles such as personal satisfaction and impact of their efforts)

THE APPLICATION FORM

Take some time to develop a good application form. Include screening questions that will save time by eliminating people who do not have the skills, availability, or knowledge to perform the tasks required. ("You mean I have to have a driver's license to take people to their doctor's appointments?") Include any required computer capabilities, particularly if you involve older volunteers, some of whom may still not be up to speed even with such basics as email.

Once, having been frustrated by volunteers who lacked basic technology skills, I threatened to add this screening question to our volunteer application form:

For the ring tone on your cell phone, did you:

a) Download a novelty ringtone from the Internet
b) Use the ringtone that came with your cell phone
c) What's a ring tone?
d) What's a cell phone?

You may also want to consider having more than one application. You could have slightly different applications for different positions, different audiences (such as corporate volunteers or interns), or different roles (one-time events or tasks versus long-term volunteer positions).

Try to keep the application as simple as possible, using checkboxes or multiple-choice options where you can. Keep the language simple and don't include unnecessary questions (do you really need to know where an adult volunteer went to high school or how many children he or she has?) or questions that ask for sensitive information such as social security numbers or driver's license numbers, unless they are required and you can protect the applicant's privacy.

Do consider questions that would help you place the volunteer (are you fluent in any other languages?) or illuminate areas of expertise (do you have any hobbies or special skills that might relate to this position?).

Try to be sensitive to diversity. Do not ask age, marital status, race, or religion (or gender, for that matter). If you use this kind of information for demographic purposes, collect it after the volunteer has been given an assignment. Use the terms "emergency contact" or "spouse or partner" rather than "husband/wife." Ask about health restrictions only as they relate to the particular position.

You will want to develop a list of red flags—responses that trigger further questions or even remove the applicant from consideration. Here are some things I consider red flags on an application for a volunteer position:

- A mature adult who has never done volunteer work before. (Never? Not even PTA or scouts? Nobody is that busy, in my opinion.)
- A person who lists so many current activities and volunteer involvements that you must question what time they will have available.

- An applicant who has no computer skills or no access to email—unless you are willing to communicate exclusively by phone and snail mail.
- An applicant for a long-term assignment who lists a string of short-term volunteer positions (may indicate either someone who loses interest quickly or someone who gets let go quickly, neither of which is a good quality in a volunteer).
- An applicant who has had no previous involvement with the organization. (What makes the person suddenly interested to the point of donating time?)
- An applicant who has poor communication skills or is not comfortably fluent in English (unless you are in need of people who speak languages other than English).
- An applicant who is defensive, angry, or unpleasant. (If the person is this way in an interview, imagine how he or she will be when brought onboard!)
- An individual who clearly is applying for a volunteer position only because he or she hopes to get a paid position. (You can sometimes benefit from the brief availability of someone who is temporarily unemployed. However, if you are looking for a loyal, long-term volunteer, that will not be this person.)

Finally, it never hurts to get a legal opinion on your application form to make sure that you haven't included any illegal questions or violated any labor laws.

SCREENING/THE INTERVIEW

Some groups are so desperate for volunteers that the screening process consists only of checking to see if the potential volunteer has a heartbeat; however, if you have done your recruiting well, you may actually have some people to choose from, and it really does pay to screen volunteers.

The interview is a way not only to find out more about the volunteer and whether he or she has the skills and knowledge necessary for the position, but also to judge how well the volunteer will fit within the organization, its culture, and the work environment. It is also an opportunity for you to convey the importance of the organization's mission and make the volunteer want to donate time to it.

When employers interview candidates for a paid job, they generally have a specific and clearly defined (relatively rigid) position description and required set of skills, knowledge, and capabilities. When you interview candidates for volunteer positions, you can be more flexible. Unless you have only one specific volunteer position to fill, you are looking for people who can help support the paid staff in achieving the goals outlined during the planning process. For this reason, you are interviewing each person to see if that person is a good fit for the organization in general, not necessarily for one specific position. Ideally, you will end up with a number of qualified volunteers who fit both the organization and its volunteer needs.

Start out by thanking applicants for their interest. Act as if they are offering you a valuable donation, because that is exactly what they are doing. Begin the interview by putting candidates at ease and building rapport. Welcome them and make a little initial small talk about the weather or some other neutral topic. Avoid comments about the person's appearance, even compliments, as they may embarrass applicants rather than put them at ease. A location where you can talk at a table or in facing chairs (rather than talking over a desk) can make the interview seem less threatening.

Be courteous and actively listen to the candidates talk, taking notes so that you don't forget which candidate said what. Do not interrupt the interview to take phone calls or speak with other people unless absolutely necessary. Remember that the candidates are interviewing you as well. It is ultimately the volunteer's decision—not yours—whether he or she joins the group.

During the interview, ask about anything that sticks out on the application form, such as gaps in work history or short service periods for other volunteer groups. Indications of potential problems include signs of inflexibility or a hidden agenda, unreasonable expectations or demands, and poor people skills (unless the position does not require personal interaction).

Look for broad types of capabilities such as public speaking ability, teaching experience, technology expertise, facilities knowledge, specialized skills (carpentry, sewing, nursing, gardening), foreign language fluency, or credentials (commercial driver's license, food handler certification) that could be useful to the organization.

It will help if you have an outline or a script so that you remember to ask the key questions and so that there is some consistency from interview to interview. This is particularly important if you are interviewing multiple candidates for the same position. It will be very confusing when it comes time to make a decision if you have asked each candidate different questions. Do not simply repeat questions from the application; try to get at who the volunteer is and whether that person will fit in successfully. Some possible questions to include are:

- Why are you interested in volunteering here?
- Have you used our services/been a member/participated in an event/visited us before?
- What skills do you have that you think will be of help to us?
- What is your availability?
- Have you had any paying jobs or volunteer positions that were similar to this one?
- Why did you leave your last volunteer position?
- What kinds of activities do you enjoy most?
- What words do people tend to use when describing you?
- What are the main things you would like us to know about you?
- Is there anything else you would like to know about our organization?

And the best last question any interviewer can ask:

- Is there anything I haven't asked you about that you would like to say?

Be sure to listen carefully not only to the responses, but also to how they are given and the level of enthusiasm. Allow the person to finish, encouraging complete responses rather than pat answers. Ask follow-up questions, where appropriate, even if they are just "How so?" "Can you give me an example?" or "Please tell me more." Let the candidate do most of the talking.

Include questions specific to the position such as "What do you like about working with animals?" or "How do you deal with disruptive children?" Open-ended questions ("What do you do when something doesn't turn out as you expected?") are better than closed questions ("Are you a good problem solver?"). By the way, questions such as that last one, that ask a candidate to judge his or her own characteristics, are nearly always a waste of time (would someone ever answer "no"?).

Depending on the demands of the position, you might want to throw in a role play or situational question. The question should not require knowledge of your policies or procedures, but should try to get at how the candidate would approach the situation. For example, "If you were teaching a group of teens and one of them kept texting while you were talking, what might you do?" Whether or not there is a single "right" answer, these kinds of questions can be helpful in seeing how volunteers might react to ethical dilemmas or problem situations and can provide insights about their interpersonal skills, problem-solving capabilities, and ability to think on their feet.

Remember that some people get nervous in an interview setting, which can make even a good applicant seem shy or withholding. Try to put the applicant at ease. You may want to save some questions to ask while giving a tour of the facility, which can be distracting and make the individual feel more relaxed.

It is better to determine a volunteer is not suited for a position during the screening process than after you have invested time and money in training, so be honest when discussing the assignment with the applicant. If you are expecting the person to perform clerical work in addition to the other volunteer tasks, be sure that is understood. If everyone in the group is expected to assist with fundraising, say so. If weekend duty is required, spell that out. Is attendance at meetings mandatory? Do work schedules sometimes have to be changed at short notice? Is public speaking required? Are volunteers expected to drive to other locations as a part of their duties? Try to anticipate anything that might be a barrier or an unanticipated part of the position and clearly state it up front to avoid disappointment down the road.

Increasingly, organizations are requiring background checks, child abuse clearances, and other legal screening tools. Explain the requirements, provide information on how to obtain them, and tell the applicant whether the volunteer must pay for them.

This is a good time to emphasize the importance of dependability. If you require volunteers to be at a certain place at a certain time, explain how this works and why it is essential that volunteers show up on time. Some people are very casual about appointments and think that because they are not being paid, they can come and go as they please. Let volunteers know you are counting on them and explain that if their schedules do not allow for firm commitments, they may need a different placement. If you have a policy that covers treatment of no-show or late volunteers (warning after two instances and dismissal after three instances, for example), spell this out now.

Be sure to have the applicant meet with more than one person at the organization. This ensures that the volunteer workforce doesn't represent the vision of a single individual. No matter how broad-minded the recruiter is, people by nature have preferences and prejudices that affect their judgment, and by getting input from others, there is less chance that a good volunteer is missed (or a bad volunteer is accepted!). Using multiple interviewers also gives you a way to evaluate how well the applicant will interact, both within the group and with the public, and gives the applicant a sense of the culture within the organization.

Choose a diverse set of interviewers, both demographically (age, gender, race) and in terms of position or area of expertise. For example, you may want to include a staff member, a board member, and another volunteer. You can also have different people focus on different aspects such as computer skills, interpersonal relations, knowledge of the group's subject matter, and so on. If possible, have the interviewers meet with the candidate individually, rather than as a panel that might seem like the Spanish Inquisition to someone not used to being grilled.

It can be particularly helpful to have someone who is serving in the same volunteer capacity interview the candidate. This gives the candidate a chance to ask questions directly of the person who knows the most about the position and will give you feedback from a person who should be a good judge of what characteristics a successful applicant should have. The relative equality of this exchange also invites a more candid discussion than does a meeting between the candidate and the person who will serve as the "boss."

Above all, make sure that between the application and the interview, you have covered everything you need in order for the candidate to understand the requirements of the position and for you to make an informed decision. You don't want to get to the volunteer's first day of work and have him or her say "You mean I have to _____? Nobody told me that!"

Conclude the interview by thanking the candidate for his or her time. Then offer the position, turn the candidate down, or explain the process that will follow (the committee will meet, a letter will be sent, someone will call, etc.).

For a volunteer position in which you will be investing time and money for training, you may want to take the time to call a reference or two. While few people will list someone they expect will say something negative, listen carefully for anything that is left out or for faint praise. Confirm the dates and positions the applicant listed on the application, and be wary of any candidate that misrepresents his or her paid work or volunteer history. You may want to start with a general statement such as "Tell me a little about Jane and what she did for your organization." It will help you get to know an applicant by hearing what qualities the referral source chooses to mention. Then ask specific questions. Try to phrase them in a way that prevents a rote response. If there are specific traits that are necessary (e.g., patience), be sure to ask about that.

Not so good: "Was Jane a good volunteer?"

Better: "Did Jane always show up on time for her volunteer shift?"

Not so good: "Is Tom capable with the computer?"

Better: "Did Tom work with the PastPerfect program?"

You may also want to ask if the referral source would rehire the volunteer if he or she asked to return. Any equivocation here should be a red flag.

When designing the screening process, make it commensurate with the demands of the position. The hiring of a long-term volunteer in a key position requires a more intensive process than the hiring of an event volunteer who will work for four hours on a single day. Do not make the process so extensive and intimidating that you lose good volunteers.

Do not be afraid to reject an applicant. A volunteer who is not a good fit, or worse, one that could become a problem volunteer, is best eliminated at this stage, when neither party has made a significant investment. This can be done either at the conclusion of the interview or through a follow-up letter that thanks the applicant for his or her time and states that you are unable to offer a volunteer position at this time (or that there are no suitable openings). Do not be pressured or made to feel guilty about turning down an applicant that is ill suited to the position or the group.

ORIENTATION

Orientation should actually begin during the recruiting process. If you have made clear the expectations, skills required, and tasks that will be performed, orientation (and volunteer service) will go much more smoothly for both the volunteer and the manager. At a minimum, you should answer the questions "What will I be doing?" "How do I do it?" "How much time will it take?" and "Can I do it my own way?"

Orientation should be designed to make volunteers feel at home as quickly as possible. It should include a tour of the facility and introductions to key staff and volunteer personnel. Point out the location of restrooms, food services, parking, office equipment, and a place to secure personal items. If the volunteer will be using any office equipment, phone systems, or computers, these should be identified and explained. Use of complex equipment or software programs should be covered during training.

Make up cards with clear, concise instructions, with illustrations if necessary, for any machinery (such as a copier) volunteers will be using or activities (such as preparing a mailing) that they will be doing repeatedly.

Make the print large so that people can read it easily, and keep the wording simple and concise. You can also do this for phone scripts, emergency procedures, frequently asked questions, or information often requested by visitors.

Orientation is when the volunteer signs any required paperwork such as the policy statement. A policy statement is a formal document that outlines the ways in which an organization intends to conduct its affairs. It may cover beliefs or core values, provide an overview of general guidelines, outline limits of authority, and clarify basic rules the group is run by. The policy statement might include the organization's position on diversity, alcohol and drug use, dress code, confidentiality, and so forth (see Chapter 6). Some organizations use individual policies for each topic rather than a general policy statement.

You may want to require volunteers to re-sign the policy statement each year. This ensures the volunteer's continued understanding of the policies and also makes sure all volunteers have signed the current statement, in case policies have changed.

Some organizations also use a volunteer agreement that defines the working relationship between an organization and its volunteers, and outlines what the expectations are for the volunteer's performance. A volunteer agreement is generally the position description or an expanded version of it.

A volunteer agreement may also include official permissions, releases, and acknowledgements. These may include any of the following:

- Confidentiality (of patient records, for example)
- Use of photos/video/audio
- Permission for background checks and clearances
- Reference verifications
- Medical treatment permission
- Hold harmless release
- Use of organization materials, information, or funds
- Conflicts of interest
- Dress and conduct codes
- Agreement regarding substance abuse testing

Orientation is when you give volunteers the basic instructions for performing their assignments. This should include an orientation package consisting of a volunteer manual and any ID badges and other instructions and materials they will need. Try to be as comprehensive as possible when gathering information and providing instructions.

You cannot be too specific when it comes to instructions for volunteers. Maxine Gaiber, Executive Director of the Delaware Center for Contemporary Arts, asked one volunteer to not wear jeans while giving a tour. She complied. She wore shorts.[3] Mary Vaughan, Volunteer Coordinator for the mobile medicine (MobileMed) ministry at the Episcopal Church of the Ascension in Gaithersburg, Maryland, called on her military background when creating her "Duties of the Volunteer" instructions. "It's painfully detailed," she says. "It's horrible to read because it tells them what to do every second. 'This is what you do, this is how you do it, this is where it's kept' ... and it repeats itself."[4]

Vaughan may call it painful, but my guess is that her volunteers thank her for it. The more common mistake is to assume knowledge the volunteer doesn't have. Most people are shy about asking for help. How much nicer to have those questions answered in a comprehensive set of instructions. "It can be easy for staff to, in their heads, simplify the project because they are working on it day in and day out," explains Tia Milne, Volunteer Manager for Northern Illinois Food Bank, "and then they can sometimes get used to just using their lingo and so volunteers who are there for the first time ... they might not know what that means." Milne says that staff must understand that volunteers may not be familiar with things they think are "the easiest in the world."[5]

Even if you don't expect volunteers to have exposure to other parts of the organization, make sure they have at least a basic knowledge of it. This helps them better understand your organization and will help them accurately describe it to others.

If you will not be in direct contact with the volunteer on an ongoing basis, set up a meeting after a month to assess progress and answer questions. The direct supervisor should monitor the new volunteer frequently during the first few weeks.

Even one-time volunteers (for an event, for example) deserve some orientation. You may want to send an information package in advance and answer any questions well before the big day. This package should include information such as when to arrive, where to check in, what the tasks will be, how to dress, whom to call in case of a last-minute emergency, as well as general information on the organization and its mission. When the volunteers arrive, provide a brief orientation and review the instructions.

HANGING ON TO THE NEW RECRUITS

So you've recruited and selected the volunteers, perhaps even trained them, but they're starting to disappear. Many a slip twixt the cup and the lip, as my mother would say.

One of the best ways to prevent volunteer drop-off is through bonding. When people feel that they are a part of a group, they are much more likely to stay with it, remain active, and donate their time (and even money) to it. For one thing, they feel more obligated to help when they feel a sense of ownership. For another, people are on their best behavior when they know others are watching (just watch people's driving skills improve when a police cruiser glides by).

The bonding process starts from day one. Do you have volunteers from the same geographic areas? Make sure people within each area meet each other. They already have at least one thing in common!

Lynn Spreadbury works with volunteers who come from different parts of the country and have to spend anywhere from a week to six months with people they've never met at a Save the Children site overseas. To get the team started, she sends out a form for them to fill in that includes questions such as "If you could see any band in concert, live or deceased, which would you go see?" and "What's your guilty pleasure?" She also asks them to include a story about themselves and a photo. "Just things to give a little bit of color to who these people are and what they're like," she explains.[6]

Make sure there is at least one person that the volunteer feels comfortable asking those "stupid" questions that we all feel we have when we're new and haven't quite caught on to how things work. This person should make sure that the new volunteer is supported during this critical early phase.

Consider a mentoring program. Pairing a new volunteer with an experienced one helps pass on knowledge but also creates a relationship. Having someone to ease the way and answer questions puts the newbie at ease and gets him or her feeling a part of things much more quickly.

One of the most successful ways to create a bonding environment is to create teams, each with its own leader, who should be an experienced volunteer. Teams can be created during orientation so that they can continue when it comes time to work on projects.

You can also help volunteers bond by providing time to socialize. Consider a potluck event, a picnic, or some other casual get-together. Provide a half hour before general meetings for people to talk to each other. Events that allow volunteers to bring a guest offer several advantages. Including nonvolunteers telegraphs that the event is for fun, not business, but allows family members and friends to learn a little more about the group and what the volunteer is doing. This helps make families more supportive of the volunteers' time away and may even bring new volunteers into the fold.

RECORDKEEPING

The first step toward measuring the impact of a volunteer program is recordkeeping. This includes tracking volunteer time, project accomplishments (impact), revenues raised (if applicable) and any other measures unique to your program area. These statistics can be used to demonstrate to funders, donors, board members, and the general public that you are maximizing the effectiveness of your efforts through volunteers rather than relying solely on paid staff. You can even convert volunteer time to a dollar value to show the importance of volunteer efforts.

A variety of volunteer management software programs, online services, and cloud-based systems provide ways of scheduling, tracking, recording, and measuring the impact of volunteer programs. If your organization has one of these systems, make sure you are familiar with all the features it offers and maximize its usefulness. If it allows volunteers to enter their own information, you will need to provide some training for this so that the information they provide is accurate and consistent. Online systems have the benefit of being available from multiple locations. Some also allow you to tabulate the information, run reports, and export data. They vary in how easy they are for volunteers to use.

If you do not have access to an automated system, time sheets are a simple way to record hours. You can create a form that each volunteer uses to document his or her own hours or have a sign-in sheet where volunteers sign in and out on a master sheet. Whichever you choose, be sure to capture the information and save it in a way that gives you information you can use in evaluating volunteers, determining how much time certain tasks take, creating effective schedules, and recognizing volunteers who reach service milestones.

Your recordkeeping tool should be as simple as possible while still giving you information you will actually use. Do not require volunteers to enter specifics you do not need (such as timing individual tasks, or recording phone calls or bathroom visits).

Looking at volunteer time records can help you identify time sinks (tasks that take more time than they are worth), areas that need more attention, tasks that should be given to a paid staff member, tasks that should be outsourced or made more efficient, tasks that should be mechanized or computerized, and volunteers who are struggling. Taking the time to review these statistics will help you improve the efficiency and productivity of the volunteer program.

EVALUATION OF VOLUNTEERS

Volunteers appreciate—and deserve—feedback on how they are doing. Everyone feels unsure when doing something new, and having a mechanism in place to evaluate volunteer performance can provide a way to accomplish this. It also gives you a way to correct mistakes that occurred during the screening, training, or position assignment process. Evaluating volunteers and giving them advice on how to improve their effectiveness helps volunteers do a better job and allows the organization to use its volunteers more effectively. Permitting volunteers to perform poorly does no one good.

Volunteers, because they are donating their time and working for no financial compensation, often expect to be treated differently from paid workers. For this reason, respect for this contribution and recognition of their special status should be a part of any evaluation process. However, you may need to reinforce that professional standards are still expected, as are essentials such as reliability, honesty, and cooperation.

You may want to start with a self-evaluation. Ask the volunteer to fill out a questionnaire that focuses on their strengths and weaknesses, and the performance of the tasks that were described in the position description. If the volunteer was asked to set personal goals, the progress toward those goals can be evaluated as well. The questionnaire can also include questions that address the volunteer's level of satisfaction, which will make the evaluation more of a two-way street.

Depending on the type of volunteer program, you may want to set up an evaluation milestone at one week, one month, six months, one year, or some combination of these. These evaluations do not have to be the same. For example, a one-week evaluation may be as simple as a casual interview to determine how the volunteer is coping and to offer minor corrections and words of encouragement, whereas an annual evaluation might be a written report filed by the volunteer's supervisor that compares the worker's performance against the position description and any goals that were set (not unlike an employee review).

Some groups use a trial period for new volunteers. This allows both the volunteer and the organization to "test drive" the arrangement without having to make a commitment. In this case, the evaluation becomes a time to decide whether the arrangement is working, needs to be tweaked in some way, or is not working and the volunteer should be released.

Evaluations are a good time to take another look at the match between the volunteer and the position. Be alert for situations in which the volunteer has cherry picked—taken on the desirable tasks but ignored the others. Also watch for task creep.

Task creep is when the volunteer ends up doing tasks not in the position description. Sometimes, this occurs when tasks should have been part of the position description but were inadvertently left out. Other times, additional tasks that were casually assigned to the volunteer become an expected part of their position. Task creep can also occur when the volunteer expands the scope of the position. This can cause problems if the volunteer is doing tasks that someone else should be doing (possibly even a staff member) or if the volunteer is making decisions that exceed his or her authority, which can have insurance and liability repercussions in addition to creating interpersonal problems within the group.

Task creep, whether initiated by the group or the volunteer, should be examined to determine whether it is a sign that the position needs to be redefined, or an indication that the volunteer needs to direct his or her efforts on the tasks expressly outlined in the position description. Both situations should be dealt with quickly, in consultation with the volunteer.

During the evaluation, take the time to listen to the volunteer. The evaluation is a time for both of you to examine how the relationship is working out and should be a collaborative process. Resist becoming defensive—hear the volunteer out and consider what changes you can and are willing to make to provide a better experience.

Review the volunteer's accomplishments against the position description or goals, praising milestones reached and discussing where improvements can be made. This is also a time for the volunteer to bring up any issues such as additional resources needed, modifications to time schedules, or changes to tasks being performed.

If there have been problems with the volunteer's performance, you must confront the volunteer for the benefit of the individual as well as the group. Be clear and specific about what you want changed. Avoid personal criticisms and don't be vague; focus on the tasks and the way they are being done rather than on personal characteristics. For example: "This position requires the volunteer to open the front door and be ready to receive patrons at 9 am," not "You are not very punctual" or "You have a bad attitude."

Consider that there are many possible explanations for poor performance. Here are some possibilities:

- Unclear or incomplete instructions
- Inadequate training
- Lack of necessary resources
- Lack of required skills or knowledge
- Illness/personal problems/psychiatric conditions

- Difficulty understanding instructions (can be due to illiteracy, learning disability, vision or hearing problems, stress, attention deficit syndrome, poor English comprehension, or other problems)
- Physical or mental limitations
- Job or family demands
- Substance abuse
- Financial problems, undependable transportation, or unpredictable schedule
- Lack of motivation

Ask the volunteer for ideas about how performance can be improved. You are looking for specific actions, not just "I'll try harder." Sometimes, this discussion will uncover the fundamental problem, which may be correctable.

You may want to set specific goals and evaluate the volunteer against those goals. Dan Gabor, Regional Field Director for Organizing for America PA, suggests making sure goals are realistic. "If you set a goal that is, for someone, unreachable, their first reaction is that I can't do this . . . take those goals and break them down and say 'Well, we might not be able to do this, but this is how we're going to try to.'"[7] You can always raise the goals as they gain experience and confidence.

EVALUATION BY VOLUNTEERS

Volunteers appreciate—and deserve—a chance to voice their opinions about how things are run. They particularly should have a say in how the volunteer program operates. This input will help tell you what is working and what needs to be changed so that you can build a more successful program and be able to attract more volunteers.

Survey the current volunteers to find out what they wished they had known when they started, what they think are the most important things for volunteers to learn, and what problems they had had that might be prevented through proper training. Get their ideas for alternate ways of performing tasks, new projects that could be undertaken, or more efficient ways to organize systems. Solicit input on meeting topics, training, orientation, and evaluation.

Provide opportunities for volunteers to offer input at key points in their experience, because people forget quickly and you will get more valuable feedback if you ask for it when the experience is fresh. For ongoing evaluations, you can either use the volunteer's anniversary (the end of their first year of service, for example) or survey the entire group at the same time each year. If you have a group that is on the same schedule (they went through training together or started work together), the first option may work, but if you take volunteers on an individual basis, a group survey is more manageable and easier to make anonymous.

Evaluations must be anonymous if they are to yield honest information. Either use paper surveys that can be dropped into a box or use one of the online survey tools such as Survey Monkey or Zoomerang. Even with this method, you may hear largely what people think you want to hear, but people will be more honest than they would when talking with you face-to-face.

After you tabulate the data, share key points with the volunteers. Even negative feedback should be shared. This accomplishes two things: it lets volunteers know that the process is fair (you didn't sanitize the results), and it gives you an opportunity to acknowledge the problem and explain what changes you will make to address it.

Which brings me to something you should consider before sending out the survey: don't ask for input if you don't intend to act on it. Nothing will discourage people more than giving them the illusion that they have a say in how things are done and then ignoring their input. Say, for example, you are considering a gift for volunteers. You might ask "Which of the following gifts would you appreciate most?" followed by a list of gifts you are willing to provide. Do not ask the open-ended question "What gift would you like?" because you will likely get responses that are impractical or unaffordable. Likewise, do not include options that you are not prepared to provide. And if you have already made a decision, don't ask for input as if you are open to suggestions!

Don't forget ask them to evaluate you. Include a question or two about how meetings are run, how the program is organized, whether volunteers feel their training was sufficient, and so forth. Do not assume that you are above improvement.

Evaluating the volunteer program also gives you the opportunity to remind volunteers why their contributions count. Report successes when they happen and provide an overview annually (I used to call this my "state of the union address").

MEASURING RESULTS

Everything that can be counted does not necessarily count; everything that counts cannot necessarily be counted.

—Albert Einstein[8]

Accurately measuring the impact of a volunteer program is difficult, but it is important to try for the following reasons:

- It demonstrates to funders, management, members, the board, staff, front-line volunteers, and constituents that the volunteer program makes an important contribution, both to the organization and to the community.
- It provides proof of success that encourages funding sources to support the program.
- It encourages people to volunteer by substantiating the effectiveness of the organization, and hence the impact that their volunteer efforts would have.
- It educates the media and the private, public, and nonprofit sectors about volunteering.
- It provides information that you can use to improve the volunteer program and benefit the people who volunteer.

Results can be measured in terms of numbers of volunteers, volunteer hours contributed, and number of constituents served. You can also tabulate specific accomplishments (number of veterans counseled, patients visited, meals delivered, etc.). In some settings, you can also attempt to measure satisfaction levels among your organization's constituents or clients.

Here are some common ways in which managers of volunteers measure success:

- Number of volunteers
- Length of service/lifetime hours of service
- Volunteer hours/value of time donated
- Money/in kind donations made by volunteers
- Money/in kind donations raised by volunteers
- Contacts made
- Comparisons with other branches of the same organization or with other organizations
- Professional evaluation from outside consultant
- Measurement against own standards (goals in plan)
- Cost/value or cost/benefit
- Turnover ratio

- Surveys of clients/community
- Clients served/clients satisfied

The last two factors attempt to measure success by how the recipients of the volunteer services (the customers, as it were) feel about the program and the services they received. This is usually done through client satisfaction surveys or interviews with random clients. Measuring success by client perception is important because it is possible that volunteers could be happy with their roles, having a quantifiable impact (in terms of hours served or clients reached), but not providing services the clients want or not providing them in an optimal manner. Client surveys can also uncover unmet needs, opportunities for new programs or services, and problems with the way services are being provided. This also shows clients you view them as partners, with a shared interest in the organization's mission.

If you cannot directly survey clients, consider including client impact questions on your volunteer surveys. Questions such as "How satisfied do you think our clients are with the services we provide?" or "Have you heard any comments from clients that would help us improve our services or the way we deliver them?"

Another way to measure success is to attempt to determine the monetary value of the volunteer program. One common way of fixing a dollar amount is to calculate how many hours have been served and then multiply that by an hourly rate. This is called the wage replacement model. Independent Sector publishes a suggested rate each year (the estimated value of volunteer time for 2011 was $21.79 per hour). This figure is based on the average hourly earnings of all production and nonsupervisory workers on private nonfarm payrolls (as determined by the Bureau of Labor Statistics). Independent Sector takes this figure and increases it by 12 percent to estimate for fringe benefits.[9]

Tony Goodrow, founder of Volunteer[2], a provider of volunteer management software, argues that valuing volunteer contributions this way doesn't take into account what has been accomplished and that assigning a flat rate per hour actually leads to bad management practices. "If the hours are down, by let's say 25 percent, it doesn't look as good," Goodrow explains, "as if they were up 25 percent; however, what is not taken into consideration is what got accomplished. So if the same things got accomplished from one year to another, and we had fewer volunteer hours to make that all possible, that ought to be rewarded, because we've managed the hours that were donated to us, that we just spent, more effectively."[10]

Goodrow prefers a variation he calls the "scarce resources model." This model looks not at the value of the time it took to accomplish a task, but at the value of the task that was accomplished. "We can put value on the volunteer hours related to what it might be if you had to pay someone to do that function," he says. "But then we need to put a value on the output of what gets accomplished."[11] He suggests that organizations look at what rates commercial entities are charging for similar services. For example, if the organization uses volunteer accountants to do tax returns for people who can't afford to get them done, focus on the value of the tax returns completed, using the standard fee a company like H&R Block might charge, say $50 a tax return, rather than using an hourly rate. If volunteers drive seniors to their doctors' appointments, use the standard taxi fare in your city.

Goodrow equates volunteer time with donors' money. "Volunteer time and money are both scarce resources. In economic terms, that doesn't mean that we can't find them, it means that there are limitations to how much is in the pool. So we have to choose how we want to spend each dollar because you can't spend it twice and we have to choose how we use the volunteer time that's being bestowed us. They are the same thing—scarce resources."[12]

If something is not commercially available, he advises making a best guess. To help illustrate how to set a value, Goodrow uses this example: Say you are a hospital volunteer manager. Would you rather have the volunteer's time to do 1,000 hospital visits or a $1 million donation? You would probably take the million dollars, and so Goodrow makes the same offer except it's half a million dollars. He keeps cutting the amount, and eventually you will take the visits. Then, using simple arithmetic, you have a value for what that visit is worth. "It's very ambiguous," he says, "but that's OK because the way this measurement is used is most typically comparing last year to this year and next year or comparing one hospital in a chain to another hospital within that same chain—that's very important—so even though there's some ambiguity in some of the numbers used, those ambiguous numbers are constants in the comparisons so we don't have to get too hung up on how precise that number might be."[13]

Susan Ellis doesn't like the wage replacement model either. "The problem is that that [the per-hour estimate] is a very limited way to value volunteer service. In other words, it's a mathematical calculation of wage replacement cost, but *value* is a much stronger word." She uses the example of Big Brothers/Big Sisters. "The activity, if you look at the wage replacement cost, would be like a babysitter or youth worker . . . but that is not the value of it . . . the relationship changes when it is freely given as opposed to 'it's my job to take you to the ballpark.' " Ellis says that the wage replacement model "really makes volunteers a commodity that we could either pay for or not pay for, depending. And it doesn't take into account how important some other elements are."[14]

No matter what method you use to value volunteers' contributions, it's important that you do try to value it. Just like a corporation that values its assets, you can place a dollar value on the volunteer program to give management, funding sources, and the public a real appreciation for the benefits you are providing to the community. However, it is important to remember that the monetary value provided by volunteers isn't *saving* the organization money; it's allowing the organization to use its funds to *accomplish* more.

QUESTIONS TO GET YOU STARTED

1. Do you have position descriptions for all volunteer assignments?
2. Does your application effectively screen out unqualified candidates and provide enough information to judge a candidate's potential?
3. Who (other than yourself) should interview applicants?
4. Is there an interview question that would help you identify particularly good volunteers?
5. What could be added to your orientation program to help a new volunteer become acclimated more quickly?
6. What measurements would be most useful in evaluating the volunteer program?

CHAPTER 4

Training

Get the best people and train them well.

—Scott McNealy[1]

DEVELOPING A GOOD TRAINING PROGRAM

Before starting to train volunteers, take some time to think it through. Go back to the plan and think about what kind of volunteers you need and what they need to be able to do. How will they fit into the organization and what must they know to be able to be as effective as possible? Are there opportunities to "train the trainer" (teach some volunteers how to teach others)?

Start by evaluating the skills and experience the trainees already have. What are their backgrounds? Have they received prior training? How familiar are they with your content area (hospice, animal management, children's soccer, art history, etc.)? How fast or slow should the pace be? Do you want to train them as a group or individually?

Next, consider what the volunteers need to know. This includes understanding the organization and its mission, learning how to perform necessary tasks, and knowing how to complete any recordkeeping or evaluation requirements. You will also need to identify any specialized training required. For example, if volunteers will be interacting with children, they should undergo youth protection training to help them learn how to recognize, prevent, and report abuse.

Finally, consider the best way to convey the information the volunteers need. People absorb information in different ways. Some people learn better when the information is presented visually, while others prefer to listen or learn with hands-on activities. Some volunteers may appreciate information in graphic form rather than text. Instead of just a listing of resources, Tia Milne uses maps. One shows where supplies are located, and another indicates where safety materials and equipment are stored. If the task is complex, break it down into steps or components.

You may also want to take into consideration the ages of the volunteers. If you are working with older adults, they may have longer attention spans but need information presented slowly, clearly, and at sufficient volume to be heard well. A younger crowd may appreciate more technology and short bursts of information but if their attention lags, they may be sneaking peeks at the ball scores or texting friends.

The most effective training programs use more than one method of teaching. For example, you may combine a PowerPoint presentation (seeing and hearing), with hands-on exercises or shadowing (experiential). Keep in mind that some volunteers may be more comfortable with new technology than others, and it is more important that the training session be an effective teaching tool than a high-tech cinematic extravaganza. There are many simple yet creative and memorable ways to teach new concepts. Options include:

- Role plays or skits
- Storytelling
- Mentoring
- Shadowing
- Humor
- Panel or group discussions
- Hands-on activities
- Team exercises
- Lunch & learns
- Games or puzzles
- Demonstrations
- Video clips
- Online interactive training programs
- Webinars
- Conference calls
- Whiteboards or smart walls

- Small group sessions
- Personal stories or testimonials by volunteers or constituents
- Contests or challenges

Training volunteers as a group may benefit the volunteers as well as make life easier for you. According to experts on education, "Much learning occurs in groups and among individuals engaged in tasks together."[2]

If you do decide to work with a group, you may want to take advantage of opportunities to have them train in teams, which not only assists with their learning, but also helps them form friendships that will help them bond to the volunteer program. This approach also allows you to assign a small team project to help cement the material taught.

The team project can be an actual volunteer assignment to be completed after training ends, or it can be an exercise held during the training session. For example, you might give each team the same assortment of odd objects (play dough, marshmallows, paper, crayons, toothpicks, paper cups, buttons, etc.) and ask them to put together a short lesson on a concept they've learned. This usually generates a lot of camaraderie and fun, while forcing them to repeat information they've learned. Give them a set period of time to develop their lesson (15 minutes or so) and then ask for a one- to two-minute presentation. Any mistakes can be corrected gently, as in "Love what you did with the marshmallows, but remember that . . . "

In designing the training program, don't forget to include the big picture. During training, show the volunteers how their efforts help accomplish the organization's goal. Dan Gabor advises "being able not only to explain the how but also the why. So not only this is how we knock on doors and this is how we talk to voters, but this is why we do it."[3]

Look within your community for resources that might help you train volunteers. For example, business executives might teach volunteers public speaking skills, professors from a nearby university might provide educational content in your subject area, and teachers might give volunteers tips for working with children.

Be sure to cover any specific expectations that may or may not be obvious to the volunteer. For example, training for volunteers who deliver meals or medical services to homebound individuals should include gaining an understanding of the need to be reliable and punctual. In addition to specific position functions, cover basic tasks such as using office supplies and answering the phone, as well as issues relating to professionalism such as appropriate dress and how to greet clients.

Make sure you cover authority limitations, even if this is covered in the policy statement or volunteer agreement. Items to cover include whether volunteers can purchase or order materials, sign correspondence on behalf of the organization, speak to the press, sign contracts or liability releases, drive vehicles in performance of their work, have direct contact with clients, have full building access, have keys or security codes, make exceptions to policies, recruit and hire other volunteers, make their own hours, change schedules for themselves or other volunteers, contact board or staff members, and so forth.

Large organizations may need several different training programs. Jim Starr explains how the American Red Cross training program works: "Someone who expresses interest in becoming a Red Cross volunteer goes through our intake process—gets interviewed, we determine what their areas of interest are, what their skill sets are, and then we try to put them into a track. For instance, we have volunteers who are trained in shelter management and bulk distribution, mass care and feeding, in case work, and things of that nature. Where a volunteer is placed is driven by what their particular area of interest is, what our needs are in terms of where we need volunteers, and what skill sets they bring to the table."[4]

If you have long-term volunteers, you may find it necessary to update training to address organizational changes, new policies and procedures, and changes in technology. Meghan Kaskoun, Volunteer Manager for the Aronoff Center for the Arts, Cincinnati Arts Association, had some volunteers that had been with the organization since it started 17 years earlier. Since that time, the program had gotten more structured and there were new guidelines. As a result, the older volunteers were doing one thing and the newer ones were doing another. She found a gap in perception between the two groups and shared this fact with the volunteers. She held a mandatory training session for anyone who had received orientation during the first two years. "We allowed them to sit at some round tables and give us suggestions for things that were most often complained about ... they were able to brainstorm some ideas and we were able to implement some really good communication ideas and some training ideas from those sessions." Kaskoun used the information to create a report, which she presented to the volunteers. In the report, she thanked them for participating and outlined "here's what we did with your information, here's what we can implement right away, here's what we can't ... and here's why."[5]

Although many people hate tests, they can be a good way to measure whether people have learned the material you have presented. More important, they can actually help people learn. By giving a test and then allowing participants to correct their own papers, the volunteers can see their mistakes and learn the correct responses. This helps reinforce the information.

In planning any orientation or training, consider the question, "What would someone need to know to feel comfortable and competent in carrying out this position?" The answer to that question should lead you to the design of your training program.[6]

HOW TO RUN AN EFFECTIVE TRAINING SESSION

A good learning environment starts with a comfortable room, with strong lighting, proper temperature control, and good sound. Set a friendly, casual tone that invites input and puts people at ease. Set rules up front about cellphone and computer use during sessions, and minimize external distractions where possible.

If you are training volunteers as a group, you may want to start with an icebreaker. This should not last longer than a half hour, preferably only 10 to 15 minutes. Icebreakers are simple exercises that initiate conversations and encourage participants get to know and respect each other. A good icebreaker encourages trust and cooperation but does not make people feel uncomfortable. The activity should be appropriate to the group's age level, physical abilities, and skills.

Remember to break content into digestible segments, and vary both content and delivery to avoid a high snooze factor. If you have a large block of material to present, interrupt it with a hands-on activity or demonstration. Present the most challenging content early rather than late in the program and put interactive content or tours after lunch, when participants may be inclined to be sleepy.

During the training session, allow time for questions and encourage participants to keep asking questions until they are sure they understand. If possible, provide ways for volunteers to walk through, practice, and reinforce what they have learned.

Any training program should include a handbook, training manual, or online guide that volunteers can consult later, to reinforce the learning experience and refer to as questions arise. This should contain all elements of the training program (copies of PowerPoint presentations, exercises, handouts, and answers to frequently asked questions) as well as copies of all policies, procedures, maps, releases, and other materials that were used. Volunteers also appreciate resources (websites, books, articles, organizations, social media, etc.) that they can use to help educate themselves. This resource can expand on what was taught during training by providing more in-depth and detailed information, specialized material, and step-by-step instructions for common tasks.

Be sure to use an evaluation form to get input from volunteers about your training program. You may want to ask for the evaluation form at the conclusion of training (to gauge the quality of the learning experience, comfort level, and comprehension) and again a few weeks later (to measure how effectively the training program actually prepared them for their positions).

OTHER WAYS TO TRAIN VOLUNTEERS

One of the best ways to train people is simply to model the desired behavior. This is particularly effective for teaching repetitive actions such as interviewing, political canvassing, client greeting, ticket selling, and so forth. It is also a way to convey subtleties that are difficult to describe or sensitive to discuss.

For example, suppose you have a booth at a fair and notice that volunteers are not engaging people, so no one is stopping to pick up information. You might tell the volunteers something like, "I find it helps to have an opening question to connect with people as they walk by." Then when the next person starts to walk by, use your question ("Do you have a dog? We're giving out information about the risks of Lyme disease") and begin to engage the person in conversation. This shows the volunteers how it is done without overtly criticizing their behavior.

If you work with volunteers who are particularly good at a task, use them as examples (with their permission). This can be done as role play during training but is even more effective in real situations. You may even ask a particularly effective volunteer to train others. This fosters leadership, spreads the training task around, and shows new recruits how experience will make them more confident and effective.

You may want to consider cross-training volunteers if you use volunteers for different tasks and have volunteers who would like to gain new capabilities. This way, you have more options when it comes time to fill an empty slot or find a replacement for a volunteer who calls in sick.

For complex tasks, shadowing can be an excellent training tool. Have the trainee follow an experienced volunteer through the full execution of the task, from locating any needed materials through recording any required information. This can be done as many times as it takes for the volunteer to get the hang of it. The training period is also a time to get to know the volunteers better and see how their personality and skills match up to the assignments. For example, Wings for Success provides free clothing to help women land jobs and get back on their feet. Interacting with clients requires sensitivity, empathy, and tact. So before volunteers work one-on-one with clients, Mary Pat Knauss has them shadow an experienced volunteer. "It becomes pretty clear within a couple of weeks whether or not a volunteer is well-suited for that kind of interaction," she says.[7] Those who aren't a good match are offered the opportunity to volunteer in other ways.

For some kinds of volunteer positions, it can be useful to allow trainees to experience—at least in practice—some of the situations they may face in their work. Situational training can help volunteers develop decision-making skills, build confidence, and learn to react to scenarios in ways that become second nature. This can be particularly important for training volunteers how to respond to emergency situations.

This type of training can be accomplished through developing "what if" scenarios that mimic something that has occurred in the past or something that might occur in the future. For example, for a volunteer who will be delivering meals to a homebound person, some what-if scenarios might include: what if you are asked to perform personal errands, what if the person confides domestic abuse to you, or what if the individual appears to be having a medical crisis.

If you are training people for a particularly complex volunteer position, consider creating an "apprentice" or "in training" position that the volunteer fills after initial training. In the Master Gardener program, this falls after training but before certification.

If you have the budget, videos can be used to illustrate proper and improper ways to react to the different situations. You might also consider asking paid staff or experienced volunteers to act out some scenes. Then the trainees can practice the same or similar situations as role play, which can allow you to respond in different ways to the actions of the volunteers to see how they react. After these kinds of exercises, discussion should be encouraged. How did that feel? What could you have done differently? Did you feel you had control of the situation?

Using mentors (seasoned volunteers) or buddies (other trainees) can help ease fear, spread the training task, and encourage team bonding. In our Master Gardener program, we found we were losing volunteers during and just after training. We decided to group the trainees into teams based on where they lived. Experienced Master Gardeners were selected to serve as team leaders. Their sense of ownership was reinforced by naming the teams by the leaders (Team Nick, Team Cindy, etc.). At the first training session, trainees were seated with their teams so that they would get to know their teammates first. As training progressed, the trainees realized some of the advantages of the teams on their own. Some of them car-pooled, and others met to study together. If a volunteer had to miss a training session, his or her teammates picked up extra handouts. As the teammates got to know each other, they began to realize they could depend on each other for help. Not only was there a virtually zero dropout rate for this training class, but volunteers were much more confident and engaged more quickly. Some teams developed projects they wanted to do even before their training period was complete. A year later, some of them were still working with their teams.

ADDRESSING FEARS

It is normal for people beginning any new endeavor to have a few butterflies. These may be doubts about their own capabilities (imposter syndrome); worries about the commitment, loss of free time, or additional responsibilities; or real fears associated with the work itself (exposure to injury or disease, working in a high-crime area, or dealing with potentially dangerous animals or people).

Some fears can be addressed during the training process. Acknowledging feelings of uncertainty and providing reassurance can be very helpful, but you should also provide help in building the volunteer's confidence and capabilities. Dan Gabor says he has his organizers start by talking with the volunteer to develop a bit of a relationship and to explain the importance of their work. "A lot of what it is with people, especially the first time, [is they] think that 'Oh no, I can't do this' ... It's really about investing time into training individuals and sort of breaking down barriers that they may have set for themselves. Like there are plenty of people who aren't comfortable talking with voters perhaps, but out of necessity we have to sort of get beyond that and train them to a point where they are able to step out of their comfort zones and begin doing that work."[8]

People often have the sense that others know more or are more capable than they themselves are. Providing a thorough orientation and training program can help reduce these fears, as can offering new volunteers re-sources—people or information sources to go to when they have questions or problems. This is also a time when mentors can play a big role, both to answer questions and to provide reassurance.

If the volunteer position includes some personal risk, it is best to be straightforward about it. Go over precautions the volunteer can take, secu-rity procedures the organization provides, and emergency or safety prac-tices and procedures that are in place.

TRAINING SHORT-TERM OR SPONTANEOUS VOLUNTEERS

Training short-term volunteers (who will assist at an event or on a one-time basis) or spontaneous volunteers (who show up at short notice, as in disaster response situations) requires a different approach. For these volunteer situations, preparation and organization are critical. Jim Starr explains how the American Red Cross does it: "During extremely catastrophic disasters, like Hurricane Katrina, we often see an influx of what we call spontaneous volunteers and these are individuals who haven't worked with the Red Cross before but have stepped up and said 'we'd like to help.' That presents a unique challenge in disasters because we have volunteers who want to help who haven't been trained and so we do have a process where we provide them some basic training right off the bat and then try to get them placed in positions that don't require the level of depth of training that some other functions may have."

For these kinds of volunteers, you must plan ahead and put an infrastructure in place in anticipation of their arrival. For short-term volunteers, you may want to create volunteer packets that provide all the necessary information and send them to the volunteers in advance. For events, host a walk-through a few days or a week before and invite potential volunteers to come see where they will be stationed, what they will be doing, and how the event will flow. Then be prepared to conduct a short training session on-site when the volunteers arrive at the event. You may also want to prepare a palm card or "cheat sheet" with key phone numbers, emergency procedures, and other important information.

In some situations, you may be able to anticipate spontaneous volunteers and provide readiness training. "We have a very extensive training regimen that we have our volunteers go through prior to being deployed for a disaster," says Starr, "so the bulk of our volunteer workforce that is responding to disasters are trained volunteers [who were trained] by the American Red Cross. They know what they're supposed to do, when they're supposed to do it, how they're supposed to do it, so that really facilitates a lot of our deployment and engagement of volunteers before, during, and immediately after a disaster."[9]

Another way to handle large influxes of relatively untrained volunteers is to pair them with experienced volunteers. Meghan Kaskoun had an unusually large production that required four shows a day. This meant she had to fill nearly 240 volunteer positions every day. Her normal training program started with an interview and orientation, some hands-on shadowing during a regular show, and training in emergency evacuation procedures, but there was no time for that. So she created a brief modified version of the program and invited local corporations to send teams of volunteers for particular shifts. "We positioned them only at specific positions and augmented that with our regular fully-trained ushers so that we could have the coverage we needed ... so that worked out really well ... it definitely saved our hind end in that particular instance."[10]

TRAINING AS A BENEFIT

Some kinds of volunteer positions not only require extensive training, but also result in the volunteer gaining a new credential or accreditation. In these situations, training can be positioned as a benefit of service. In other words, in exchange for volunteering their time, volunteers will gain a substantive—perhaps even marketable—skill. This aspect can be emphasized by providing a certification, specific title, or other credential that has perceived value. You may even provide volunteers with external training—send them to a workshop or professional certification program, for example.

The concept of learning a new skill or gaining a certification can be an attractive benefit for some volunteers. It can lead to paid job opportunities, a new career, or advancement within an existing career. Within the organization, there may be a path from front-line volunteer to management or board service, or to paid employment.

While this can work to the organization's advantage in terms of recruiting volunteers, it can also create problems. People may volunteer in order to get the training and then drop out of the program before they have given significant volunteer service. You can try to screen these people out during the interview process by questioning their motivations for volunteering, but it is difficult to identify people who intentionally disguise their intentions.

You may want to consider charging a fee for training (which you may or may not want to reimburse after a set period of volunteer service has been completed). This not only helps ensure at least a minimal amount of commitment from the volunteer, but also increases the perceived value of the training.

For some volunteer positions, ongoing training is required so that the individual's skills are kept sharp and knowledge is kept current. This is particularly important for positions that require someone to have the skills to be ready to act, yet may never have had to use those skills. Examples are emergency responders and disaster relief workers. These volunteers may go weeks, months, even years without having to use their skills, yet they have to be fully trained with the latest techniques and ready to go at any moment.

Advanced training is also a benefit for the organization. It ensures that both its paid staff and its volunteers are knowledgeable, capable, and confident. Susan Ellis suggests scheduling periodic in-house group discussions of current trends and issues that affect the organization or its content area and inviting anyone who's interested, whether volunteer or paid staff. She says staff members may be surprised by the level of understanding committed volunteers have about your work, particularly as volunteers may approach any topic from perspectives different from those of full-time staff. These shared discussions can also promote teamwork and better cooperation.[11]

TRAINING PAID STAFF TO WORK WITH VOLUNTEERS

You wouldn't install a new piece of office equipment without providing training or guidance to the people who will be using it. If you bring in volunteers without offering any training to members of the paid staff who will be working with them, it amounts to the same thing. If staff members and volunteers will be working together, you must take the time to train the staff to work with volunteers successfully. This is true whether or not the volunteer technically reports to you or to the staff member.

It will help immensely if staff members have been involved in the decision to use volunteers and have been involved in the planning and development of the volunteer program. Otherwise, they may feel threatened (What if someone will do my job for free?), intimidated (What if the volunteer is more capable than I am?), or put upon (Now I have to do my job *and* supervise a bunch of amateurs?). If, however, staff members understand and appreciate the benefits volunteers can bring to the organization, things will run much more smoothly.

It will also help if staff members are shown "what's in it for me." Ideally, members of the paid staff will see volunteers as a good investment (I put a little time in up front, and my job will be a whole lot easier in the end) and a resource that will make their jobs easier, not harder. What you don't want to do is push volunteers on staff members or make them feel that they need the volunteers' help because they are not doing their job well.

Paid staff and volunteers should see themselves as partners working to further the organization's mission. The paid staff should understand the value of the volunteer program and its role in the organization. It will help if you can provide opportunities for paid staff and volunteers to communicate, work together, build rapport, and cooperate. Options include informal gatherings, monthly meetings, joint problem-solving sessions, and opportunities for collaborative projects.

Staff members should treat volunteers as fellow professionals, not second-class citizens. Susan Ellis says: "There are still a lot of misconceptions about volunteers: that they're undependable, that they're not skilled, all that kind of stuff. And it's just prejudiced and not borne out by reality. But it also is a self-fulfilling prophesy. Because the organizations that assume that the volunteers are unskilled and not very committed are going to create very limited assignments so that nothing can go wrong ... and therefore what happens is they only attract people who are motivated by unimportant things."[12] Successful organizations show staff members the value their volunteers bring, develop a wide range of volunteer positions, and forge a collaborative relationship between the paid staff and the volunteers.

QUESTIONS TO GET YOU STARTED

1. What methods have worked the best for training the kinds of volunteers you need, and what might you change to make your training program even more effective?

2. Are there any holes in the knowledge base of existing volunteers that should be addressed?

3. Are there steps you could take to better prepare for an unexpected need for additional volunteers?

4. What could be added to your training program so that it prepares volunteers more effectively for the tasks they will need to perform?

5. Can you provide any opportunities for shadowing, mentoring, or hands-on learning?

6. Do you have a program in place to help paid staff learn how to work with volunteers in an efficient and positive way?

CHAPTER 5

Organization and Communication

The secret of my success is a two word answer: Know people.

—Harvey S. Firestone[1]

MATCHING THE VOLUNTEER TO THE TASK

Matching the skills and abilities of volunteers to the appropriate tasks is one of the most important jobs you have and is key to retaining volunteers. Saddle volunteers with nothing but boring, thankless tasks or assignments that ignore their skills, and you are going to have unhappy volunteers (and you probably won't have them for long). Conversely, give volunteers tasks that are too challenging or ones they are not capable of handling competently, and they will become frustrated and unhappy.

Susan Ellis, who has been advising volunteer managers for 35 years, says: "Everything that you read about [volunteer management] is always on the subject of how do we get people to volunteer . . . The key to the entire thing is to find work that is appealing to a wide range of people but also that is meaningful and that the organization is prepared to manage."[2] She says this relates both to work design and to recruitment.

Try to provide a variety of tasks to meet the interests and skills of your volunteers. If the organization is one that works with children, have some tasks that do not require interaction with children. You may have volunteers who support the cause but would prefer office work or interaction with the children's parents. Others may have computer skills that could be put to use developing a database, creating PowerPoint presentations, or helping with the website or Facebook page. Focus on creating positions with real meaning and developing task groupings that will challenge and motivate volunteers.

Look for ways for volunteers to contribute in meaningful ways. This means both being flexible in how you structure volunteer positions and being alert to the capabilities, skills, and interests of the volunteers. A single person may be able to participate in the organization on multiple levels or through various means. For example, a volunteer might be a donor, assist with the strategic planning process, serve on the board, and participate in fundraising events. Another volunteer might help with the website, create a blog, provide graphic arts design, and write a grant proposal, all without ever setting foot inside the organization's facility.

Remember that people have different working styles. Some people are highly organized and don't feel comfortable unless things are tucked into tiny labeled compartments. These folks often make excellent project managers. Other people are blue-sky thinkers. They start sentences with "What if . . . " or "Suppose . . . " These are your go-to people for new ideas or fresh approaches. People who like to work on deadline and perform better with a little pressure may do well running events, writing grant proposals, or working on projects with drop-dead dates. Those who fall apart at the slightest pressure may do better working at their own pace, on projects that have no particular end date.

People also have different personality traits. Consider this when selecting volunteers for specific tasks. Have a volunteer with an outgoing, bubbly personality? There's your raffle ticket seller! The volunteer with a knack for putting people at ease? The perfect greeter at a health care facility. Someone who is shy? No problem for a researcher. By carefully matching tasks to volunteers' personality traits and working styles, you can increase the odds that they will be successful.

Remember to accommodate both leaders and followers. Notice the people other volunteers look up to and who seek out greater responsibility. But there are also those who are willing and able to take direction. If you don't provide clear instructions, they may sit there all day, not knowing what to do, but give them good direction, and you will have steady workers who are happy just doing a good job.

Consider whether a particular volunteer task is best done as an hourly task or as a project. Certain tasks such as museum docent or greeter must, by their nature, be assigned as an hourly task. Other tasks, such as conducting a phone survey, could easily be done at the convenience of the volunteer (and at any location). This is an important distinction because you can give project tasks to volunteers who have difficult schedules or other issues that prevent them from committing to an hourly schedule.

Project tasks are also good for volunteers with disabilities. Taking away time pressures allows them to perform tasks at their own speed and in their own way. They can utilize any assistive devices they need and perhaps even work from home if mobility is an issue.

Allow volunteers who wish to do so to build their resumes through work at your organization. Particularly during times of high unemployment, the organization may benefit from volunteer professionals such as accountants, writers/editors, computer professionals, or even people who have worked in a for-profit company that provides services similar to your non-profit organization. While you may not be able to retain these volunteers once they find full-time work, in the meantime, you are getting valuable work for free and they are able to add to their resume and show they made good use of their "down" time.

Consider volunteer events such as a cleanup day, a day of painting, or day of service (with multiple options for tasks). This approach works well for big tasks that require a lot of warm bodies (and little or no training or skills) or tasks that would normally have to occur over a long period, but with enough help could be done at one time, such as putting up a fence or putting in a garden. Entice volunteers by providing donuts and coffee, pizza, music, or other enhancements to make the task more fun. Encourage people to bring friends or work in teams.

FLEXIBLE WORK FOR FLEXIBLE TIMES

What with smartphones, virtual commuting, and people working more than one job, not to mention family pressures, it is increasingly important to be as flexible as possible with volunteer assignments. While some people may be available during "normal" work hours, others may prefer to volunteer at night, on weekends, or before their workday starts in the morning. There may also be people who would volunteer if they could perform tasks from home, perhaps even from another state or country. If you offer volunteer opportunities that accommodate a variety of schedules, then you may find it easier to attract volunteers. And if the organization provides (or could provide) services at night or on weekends, make sure you make these opportunities known to potential volunteers.

If the organization operates on a traditional 9 to 5 schedule, identify ways volunteers can contribute outside of those hours. Tasks that can be performed at home or from anywhere (virtual volunteering) include research, grant writing, website/social media help, publicity, interviewing, data entry, writing/editing, graphic design, and even traditionally in-person tasks such as mentoring. Here are some examples from the Volunteering and Service Blog at pitchin.org:

• Volunteer for Hugs and Hope, an organization that works with terminally ill children. The organization provides brief biographies of sick children, as well as their addresses. You can send a cheerful card to help brighten their day.

• If you have a website or blog, add an Amber Alert ticker. The ticker will display pictures of children who have been reported missing. You'll be helping get the message out about the child's disappearance, and perhaps someone who visits your site can help the cause.

• Utilize your talents to help a worthy organization. Offer to volunteer for a local charity by designing a website, proofreading brochures, or writing promotional material for the organization.[3]

Job sharing may be another solution. If one person can't commit to a weekly volunteer shift, maybe a team can handle it, making sure that one of them is there at the appointed time every week. Take-home work (phone calls, mailing preparation, email responses, online work) is another possible solution.

ORGANIZING VOLUNTEERS

An organized volunteer program provides a structure that ensures efficient use of the volunteers' time, assignments that advance the organization's goals, sufficient oversight, and effective follow-up. This will come about naturally as part of your strategic plan, as you move logically from the organization's goals to the programs necessary for reaching those goals and the personnel needed to get there. All that follows will be less effective if you have not laid the proper groundwork by hiring the right volunteers for the right positions, and organized them to achieve attainable goals.

Creating an environment that provides an enjoyable workplace and motivates volunteers will not only help you retain volunteers, but also attract new ones. A good organizational culture is one in which people feel secure, useful, and appreciated. Goal setting is done cooperatively, and the volunteers' ideas are welcomed. The paid staff is supportive of the volunteers, and the volunteers respect and complement the work of the paid staff. Working as colleagues, staff and volunteers work cooperatively to achieve the organization's goals.

If you have never managed people before, you may want to spend some time reading books about human resources, talking to other managers, and perhaps taking a class in management techniques. The Internet abounds with information on people management and even material specific to volunteer management. Take advantage of the resources that are available to you. What comes naturally is not always the best course of action.

One of the most important things a volunteer manager must do is organize programs and activities to make the best use of the volunteers' time. Tony Goodrow says, "I really believe that the contributions volunteers are making of their time have an incredible value to them. Just like with most organizations great care is taken to spend donated money as carefully as possible, I think we owe it to the volunteers that are donating their time that we manage their time as efficiently, effectively, and thriftily as we spend our donors' dollars."[4]

DELEGATION

When in doubt, mumble; when in trouble, delegate; when in charge, ponder.

—James H. Boren[5]

You can do everything yourself and have all of the glory (and stress, and loss of free time, and lack of fresh ideas), or you can learn to delegate. Learn to delegate. I like control too, but my life became a lot easier when I discovered delegation. And delegating means avoiding the "it's easier to do it myself" trap. Sure, it may be easier to do it yourself once, but chances are you will end up doing it again and again until you teach someone else to do it. Good organization depends upon good delegation.

No one should be indispensable. This is good for you but even better for the organization. Teaching volunteers to do things themselves—including overseeing projects and managing other volunteers—helps them grow and makes the organization stronger and more efficient. It also protects the organization against a devastating loss if you were to leave or become incapacitated unexpectedly. Creating a chain of command gives volunteers a ladder to climb and builds leadership for the years to come.

Delegation involves both delegating project or task responsibility and delegating human resources (supervisory) responsibility.

Project or task delegation involves creating a structure of project teams, activity areas, or task groupings that provide organization and a natural flow of delegated task or project responsibility. This works well for organizations that have defined activity areas (speakers bureau, outreach, fundraising, etc.). Volunteers with good leadership skills can coordinate projects and activities, and perhaps even create subgroupings for large endeavors.

You may also want to delegate specific ongoing responsibilities, such as identifying speakers or continuing education opportunities, coordinating the volunteer schedule, or managing the volunteer database to individual volunteers who show interest and aptitude for a particular task.

When you delegate a task or project to a volunteer, be clear about the parameters of what you are delegating. Be specific about what needs to be done and any time limits. Make sure boundaries of authority are clear.

Start by defining the objective (results) desired. For example, say you want to delegate the task of recruiting volunteers and setting up the schedule for a small event. You might start by saying something like, "We're getting ready for the reception and we need to make sure we have volunteers scheduled to greet guests and hand out name tags. I thought of you because you have such good people skills. Do you think you would be able to call the people on this list and put together a schedule by Friday?"

Here is what you did:

1. Stated the objective (the schedule)
2. Explained why you are delegating the task (and complimented the volunteer along the way)
3. Provided the resources necessary to accomplish the task (the list of names and phone numbers)
4. Set a deadline (Friday)
5. Stated it in a nice way (as a question/request)
6. Allowed some freedom for the volunteer (calls can be made at the volunteer's convenience, the volunteer can structure the schedule)

For more complex delegated tasks, you may want to monitor the volunteer's progress. This ensures that the project remains on track and that you aren't faced with a surprise down the road. ("Oh, you meant *registered* voters?")

Don't interfere unless absolutely necessary. Recognize that people do things differently, and there can be more than one "right" way. This can be difficult for a control freak to keep in mind, so if you tend to be controlling, whenever you feel inclined to correct a volunteer ask yourself, "Is the way he or she is doing it actually *wrong*, or just not the way I would do it?" And don't saddle your volunteers with so many instructions, guidelines, best practices, policies, and procedures that they become frustrated. If a task must be so closely defined, it should not be delegated.

At the opposite end of the spectrum from the manager who doesn't delegate anything is the manager who delegates unreasonable tasks. These are the people who like being the manager but don't like the work of being manager. "Please call these 500 people, ask them each to donate $100, then create a spreadsheet that provides demographics of the donors and convert it to a PowerPoint presentation with graphs and charts for our Board meeting Friday" is not a reasonable request of anyone. Make sure delegated tasks come with reasonable expectations.

When you set deadlines, be respectful of the fact that volunteers may be fitting their donated time in between family demands, work schedules, other volunteer work, school, and child care. Planning ahead will eliminate many deadline crunches. Remember that failure to plan on your part does not necessarily constitute an emergency on anyone else's part.

When delegating to volunteers, consider who would be the best person for the task. Don't ask people to volunteer for leadership positions during a meeting. Few people have the confidence to stand up in such a public setting. A better approach is to select someone you think would do a good job and then speak to that volunteer directly. Explain why you choose him or her and why you think the person is right for the task. Make it seem like an opportunity, not just an obligation.

Delegating supervisory responsibility allows you to reduce the number of people who report directly to you. As the program grows, this becomes increasingly important if you want to avoid being overwhelmed by email, questions, and tiny problems that could easily be resolved without your involvement. To some extent, a reporting structure will develop naturally as you create project teams or committees, each with a leader. For organizations that do not have multiple activity areas, a reporting structure can be created by grouping volunteers into teams under volunteer coordinators who have been trained to supervise other volunteers.

If paid staff members can successfully supervise the volunteers they work closest with, that will also help free you up for other activities. When volunteers work directly with or for a staff member, it makes good sense for that staff member to provide the direct supervision. This is something that you will have to work out well in advance and should be part of an overall plan from the top of the organization to integrate volunteers effectively. Staff members who provide direct supervision are better able to request (and receive) the work product they want and can ensure that the task they wanted done is being done properly.

Having staff members provide direct supervision doesn't mean you will never see the volunteer again. It is still up to you to monitor the volunteer placement, assess how the relationship between the staff member and the volunteer is working, and determine if any changes need to be made in the structure of the position or the individual placed in that position.

Staff members should have a say in how the volunteer position is structured, what training is provided, how the task is to be performed, when tasks are scheduled, and what skills and capabilities are required. Paid staff should be given the opportunity to interview prospective volunteers before they are hired for a position in their department, and staff members should have a say in whether a particular volunteer is a good fit for the position.

You may want to use a trial period as a low-risk way for all parties to test drive the volunteer placement. You will want to set up a specific date for reviewing the placement—perhaps 30 days—to give the placement a fair chance, while not forcing something that isn't working.

If supervising volunteers is a new responsibility for the staff member, you will need to be particularly supportive and alert for any need for assistance from you. This is particularly true if the individual has never had supervisory experience. Make sure you keep communication lines open, with periodic phone calls and emails to ensure things are going well. Provide praise where appropriate and be empathetic and encouraging.

Be open to both positive and negative feedback, providing advice and support as needed for dealing with problems. You will also need to have an agreed upon policy for handling grievances and terminations.

You may also want to consider creating a steering committee or advisory board if you don't already have one. This group can be of help to you in making the major decisions that affect the volunteer program and can make the volunteers feel that they have more of a voice. On the downside, I have seen these groups gain too much power and be able to essentially overrule the desires of the manager. Keep this in mind when structuring the group and make sure to clearly outline its authority and role. Select people with wisdom, experience, and creativity; avoid people with a single point of view or specific goal of their own, volunteers who have exceeded their authority in the past, and people who are motivated by increasing levels of power.

COMMITTEES

The word "committee" conjures up images of boring meetings, endless discussions, pointless deadlines, personality battles, and wasted time, but that doesn't have to be the case. One of the easiest ways to encourage volunteers to participate is to banish the old committee concept and go to project teams that focus on actions, not meetings.

The term "project team" immediately conveys the two most important elements of a successful committee: something tangible is accomplished (a project) and people work together to accomplish it (as a team). Project teams can also be smaller and more active than committees. Instead of an Outreach committee, as an example, you might have a Senior Outreach team (to target older residents), a Target Teens team (to find ways to attract teenagers), and a Community Connection team (that targets people living in the immediate vicinity). Focusing on very specific tasks also has the advantage of directing the effort toward measurable accomplishments.

If you use committees or project teams, you will need a way to select volunteers for each group. You may want to make this part of the orientation or training process by evaluating the skills and experience of the volunteers and discussing with them what kinds of activities they would like to be involved with. Then, in consultation with each volunteer, you will assign them to the specific group(s).

Another approach is to hold a meeting to present the different projects and activities. You can give one long group presentation or use a variation of speed-dating. Set up a table for each committee or project, and then number the tables. Have the volunteers count off up to the number of tables (if you have six tables, have them count to six and then start over at one). When all participants have gotten a number, have them go to the table with their number on it. The committee chair or team leader for that project should be stationed at that table, along with photos, brochures, videos, PowerPoint presentations, or whatever is best to explain in about five minutes what that group will be doing. For the remaining five minutes, the volunteers can ask questions. After ten minutes, ring a bell and have everybody rotate to the table to the left. Keep this up until the volunteers have visited every table. Place sign-up sheets for each group on a table near the door and allocate time at the end for people to sign up as they leave, once they have been to all the tables. This process allows volunteers to get to know the chair or team leader, provides a setting for asking questions in a small group setting, and adds peer pressure to help you convey the idea that everyone should sign up for at least one project or committee.

Each committee or team will need a leader. Sometimes, it is easier to get two people to share responsibility than to get one to bear the full burden. Co-chairs (or a pair of team leaders) can be a very effective way to establish leadership, providing the lines of responsibility are carefully drawn. One approach is to do as attorneys do and have a "lead chair." This means that one person is actually the head decision maker and the other takes direction from the first but then provides direction to the people on the committee. This can work well for very large projects or for situations in which an eager volunteer wants a leadership role but does not have the experience to handle the entire responsibility.

If two volunteers have equal roles, you must establish who does what in order to avoid duplication, responsibilities not being met, and general confusion. If the project or activity can be easily divided, that is the most obvious way to distinguish the roles. For example, a Master Gardener committee that handled information booths at events was split between co-chairs: one handled fairs and festivals while the other took responsibility for farmers markets. Together they organized the displays and handouts, and created a sign-out system that allowed them to share the resources in a controlled way. Co-chairs can also be used for time periods (day shift supervision and evening shift supervision, for example), volunteer type (one handles youth volunteers while another manages the adults), or facility (the same activity being managed by two people, each at a different location).

Sometimes, you must come up with a different approach to get people to take leadership roles. Dan Gabor says: "One of the best tricks is teaching people their abilities by having them figure it out for themselves." He uses the example of trying to recruit a phone bank coordinator. "Rarely will someone come in and say 'I want to be a phone bank coordinator' ... but you get somebody, you bring them in the first night, they're sitting there making calls, and you realize that they're actually pretty good at this. The next time they come in, you ask them to help you train volunteers or be that person the new person shadows, and then from there—whether this is over the course of a month or two months—you get to the point where you know that they are fully capable of running their own phone bank." Then, one time when the volunteer is working in the phone bank, Gabor says, "Oops, I've got to run out for this other meeting, can you stay here and run this?" And the volunteer is then running the phone bank. "Instead of having that escalation call in to say 'we want you to be a leader on this campaign or a leader among these volunteers,' you're able to say 'you *are* a leader among these volunteers. You've got all the skills you need to do this. It's just a title at this point. You're already doing the job.'"[6]

SCHEDULING

I am definitely going to take a course on time management ... just as soon as I can work it into my schedule.

—Louis E. Boone[7]

As you create volunteer shifts and schedules, consider the task (how strenuous or stressful it is), volunteer (age and capability), and conditions (outdoors versus indoors) and then begin to match appropriate volunteers to time slots they are willing and able to fill. You may also want to create volunteer pairs or teams that serve together. This encourages camaraderie and makes it less likely that a volunteer won't show up, as the members of the team will come to depend upon one another. If you have an ongoing activity, you may try to get volunteers to fill weekly time slots so that you don't have to create a new schedule every week.

Mary Vaughan schedules 15 to 17 volunteers to fill four shifts each week to staff the waiting room for the clinic. "We ask them [church volunteers] to sign up for one shift a month so the maximum that they're obligating themselves to is two and a half hours a month, which is pretty palatable."[8] By keeping the commitment small and well-defined, Vaughn has found it easy to attract and retain volunteers.

If you think managing 10, 100, or even 1,000 volunteers is a challenge, imagine managing 500,000. That's business as usual for Jim Starr. How does he do it? By having all the information and scheduling structure in place before the volunteers are needed. For starters, the Red Cross compiles volunteer information in a national database that the volunteers themselves can access. "We know who they are, we know what their availability is," says Starr. That way, when there is a disaster, the Red Cross can rapidly determine who is available, what skills they have, and where they can be sent. "They're required to keep their availability to deploy up to date in our volunteer management system," explains Starr, "and then basically what we do is we go through our roster and we ask our chapters to reach out to our volunteers to make sure they have updated their availability status and we go through and start deploying them."[9]

Even on a small scale, managing schedules can be daunting, but there are a few ways you can make it easier on yourself. Volunteer management software programs (see Chapter 10) offer managers a variety of ways to organize, schedule, and track volunteers. Some programs can be accessed only by management, while others allow volunteers to enter and change information.

If you don't use one of these programs, you may be able to use a password-protected area of your website or an online calendar to create the basic schedule and allow volunteers to sign up for shifts or take on specific tasks. Volunteers can then swap shifts and find a replacement if they cannot serve during a scheduled slot.

The responsibility for organizing and scheduling is increasingly being put into the hands of the volunteers themselves. For the 2012 election,

Obama for America created a smartphone app that allowed volunteers to download names of voters in their neighborhood and then report the results of their canvassing back to the campaign. "We designed our new app to help break down the distinction between online and offline organizing, giving every supporter the same opportunities to get involved that they would find in a field office," said Deputy Campaign Manager for Obama for America Stephanie Cutter.[10]

As smartphones become even smarter, they will provide an increasing number of sophisticated ways for volunteer programs to recruit skilled volunteers and allow the volunteers to schedule and manage their own activities. They will also give organizations an inexpensive and easy way to communicate with and coordinate the efforts of the volunteers.

COMMUNICATION

Communication should be open, be honest, and run in both directions. Good communication starts during the recruiting process, when you explain what the organization does, why you need volunteers, what those volunteers do, and how the volunteers and the organization benefit. Communication is critical during the orientation and training processes, when volunteers need to learn how to do their work efficiently, effectively, and safely. And communication is essential from there on out as you supervise the volunteers, ensuring that they perform well, are enjoying their work, and are furthering the goals of the organization.

Coming from an advertising and marketing background, I always try to answer the question everyone has foremost in their mind: "What's in it for me?" If you think about it, nearly every decision one makes, from which soap to buy, to what job to take, comes down to this fundamental question. If you keep it in mind, it will help you describe volunteer positions, structure recruitment campaigns, present requests for volunteer service, offer board positions, persuade staff to work with volunteers, and get your kid to do the dishes much more successfully.

Start by communicating in a positive way. This means telling volunteers more about what to do than what not to do, and more about what they can do than what they can't do. Which of the following sets of instructions would you rather receive?

You are not allowed to go into the administrator's office or the client waiting area. Do not park in any visitor spots, and do not arrive late for your shift. You cannot take a break until 11:30.

You can go into any areas except the administrator's office and the client waiting area, and can park anywhere except in the visitor spots. Clients will come to depend on you being here, so please be on time for your shift. You can take a break at 11:30.

One thing nearly all people share is the desire to be special. When you manage people, particularly when you manage a lot of people, and especially when you manage a lot of people who have the same role, it is easy to start thinking of them as interchangeable. Treat them that way and they won't stick around for long.

Call people by name and try to learn a little bit about each person, even if it's just one thing (family, hobby, interest). Remember birthdays, volunteer anniversaries, service milestones. A calendar that automatically reminds you is an excellent way to keep track of these dates. Learn how much (or how little) a sense of humor each volunteer has and find out what motivates them. Notice individual traits (enthusiasm, good sense of style, knack for fixing things) and praise them. Being aware of people's strengths not only makes the individuals feel valued, but also gives you guidance for how best to match volunteers to assignments they will enjoy and do well.

There are a variety of methods managers can use for communicating with volunteers. These include mail, phone, email, instant messaging or texting, social media, and VOIP (voice-over-Internet protocol) services. There are also online collaboration and file-sharing tools. At this writing, email is the most common way to communicate with volunteers. It's a great tool, but there are some things to keep in mind.

Email is not necessarily private. Never put anything confidential in an email. In fact, never put anything you wouldn't want someone else to read in an email. And don't use email for sensitive matters, where face-to-face communication is more appropriate, or for messages that are critical. ("You didn't get the email I sent about the bridge being out?")

In email communications, start with a clear subject line. Most people scan email subject lines quickly, so a coy or amusing subject line could easily get your email deleted, ignored, or marked as spam. Other spam flags include too many hotlinks (clickable links to websites), multiple exclamation points (or other odd punctuation), different text colors or fonts, and use of phrases such as "free gift," "special offer," and "click here."

Be specific. "Meeting" isn't very helpful to people scanning their email, whereas "Fundraising Committee Meeting" probably won't be overlooked. If the email contains essential information, put it in the subject line: "Fundraising Committee Meeting Postponed."

Be a courteous email correspondent. It only takes a moment to acknowledge receiving an email. Don't leave people hanging. Even the two letters "OK" or the phrase "got it" is better than no response at all. And remember, it doesn't take very long to type those magic words "please" and "thank you." The best advice is the simplest: read each email message carefully and make sure it says what you intended and is being sent to the correct person before you hit the irrevocable "Send."

Texting, instant messaging, Facebook, and other forms of communication are beginning to replace email. VOIP services such as Skype have made international telecommunications easy and inexpensive. These tools make for faster communication, but only if the person you are trying to reach is receptive.

Tony Goodrow says one of the biggest challenges with communicating with volunteers is "The wide range of ways in which volunteers would like to be communicated with—phone me, don't phone me; mail me, don't mail me; email me; email is passé, Facebook me—that's one of the challenges."[11] For this reason, you may want to ask volunteers the best way to reach them.

One of the best things you can do to make sure your message is heard is to limit your communications to what is actually necessary and send communications only to the people affected. For example, try to minimize the number of emails you send to volunteers. If you send too many, people will start to ignore them. Don't send every message to the entire list and don't start a "reply all" avalanche; hide the recipients if you are sending to a large group of people at once. Goodrow says: "We try to make it easy for the volunteer manager to send information to a very narrow group of volunteers so that over time those volunteers understand that when they get an email it probably has something to do with them."[12]

Although you should send people only communications that concern them, critical information should be communicated more than once, and often in more than one way (mail, email, meeting, phone calls, in person). It is easy for a single email to be lost, never read, misdirected, accidentally deleted, filtered by spam programs, and so on. Unless you receive a reply, don't assume an email has been received.

HOW TO RUN A MEETING

> People who enjoy meetings should not be in charge of anything.
>
> —Thomas Sowell[13]

A well-run meeting starts on time, ends on time, and produces decisions. Unfortunately, poorly run meetings are much more common. They start late, follow no real agenda, and end late with nothing accomplished. You *can* run productive meetings. It just takes a little planning and organization.

Start with a written agenda, preferably published in advance or at least available at the start of the meeting. When preparing the agenda, think about the logical flow of what you have to cover. If there is a controversial or complicated matter, get the easier issues out of the way first. That way you won't find yourself on item two with only five minutes left.

Make sure the room is ready (confirm room reservations at least a month in advance). Have enough chairs, arranged in the configuration that best suits the meeting, and include tables if the participants will need to take notes or do other work. If there is any chance the speaker will not be heard, use a microphone system. Set up and test all technology and check the temperature—too cold and people will be distracted and uncomfortable, too warm and people will start nodding off during the opening remarks. If people are coming from other locations, set up signage and alert front desk personnel to help them find the meeting location quickly.

Announce that you will start the meeting on time and then do so. Once you have a reputation for starting meetings on time, presto! People will arrive on time so as not to miss anything.

If you have reports to be given by different people (project team leaders, for example), list them on the agenda, along with a time allocation. Tell the presenters how much time they will be given in advance and ask them to stay within that time. If they make a good case that they need more time, you can adjust the schedule accordingly, but let them know that you will need to move on once that time has expired.

Start the meeting with an enthusiastic welcome and thank people for their time. Unless yours is a patriotic or faith-based organization, you should not open the meeting with the Pledge of Allegiance or a prayer, as these activities can make some people feel uncomfortable or even unwelcome and do not serve any purpose in a business setting (and meetings are about getting business done). Remind people to turn off electronic devices. Briefly explain the agenda and your desire to stick to the times outlined. If you have not already done so, ask someone to take notes. Introduce any special guests and then begin the announcements and proceed through the agenda, sticking to the time allotted for each item as closely as you are able.

A good way to gracefully cut off a speaker who is exceeding the time limit is a sequence of increasingly clear signals. If it's a large meeting, start by simply standing up. Then slowly move toward the front of the room. If there is a projector or podium, start to move toward it. If the lights have been turned down, start to turn them up. In smaller meetings, try to catch the speaker's eye, and indicate with a gesture that it is time to wrap up. If the speaker does not appear to be ending the presentation, interrupt at the end of a sentence or complete thought to express thanks for their excellent presentation and to ask if there are any questions. If the interruption turns out to be less graceful than you had hoped, you can always apologize and say that although you wish the speaker could continue, unfortunately, you have to cut the discussion off because of the tight schedule. In small meetings, you can simply interject something like: "Thank you, Mary. That was very informative."

Stick to the agenda unless there is reason to change the order of events. As the items are completed, check them off so that you don't skip anything. Allow time at the end for any additional items not on the agenda but have a published end time for the meeting and try your best to stick to it. Do not sacrifice a good discussion for a few additional minutes, but do not allow a meeting to go on for hours of unnecessary debate.

Try to resolve each item on the agenda. That is, there should be a resulting action item, decision reached, or task delegated. If an issue has been thoroughly discussed and no consensus seems possible, conclude the conversation. Suggest some method for moving the process forward (additional research, another meeting, involving other people, etc.) but do not waste time on fruitless discussion. Carry the item to the next meeting's agenda, but between meetings address any issues that prevented the item from being resolved.

If you have people who tend to dominate meetings, you will need to allow them to talk, but you do not have to be held captive by extended speeches. Use the "Thank you, Mary" type of interruption, while smiling and appearing appreciative but firm, and quickly call on another person or begin speaking yourself.

Do not tolerate name-calling or other signs of disrespect toward you or other people in the meeting. Acknowledge that the person feels strongly and do not discount their passion for the issue, but calmly explain that for the good of the organization (something you are all working for) you must maintain an environment that promotes a free exchange of ideas.

You may want to consider using parliamentary procedure in meetings. This sort of imposed formality sometimes causes more hard feelings than it resolves and can take away from the informal exchange of ideas, but if you are really having a difficult time maintaining control, you may wish to appoint a parliamentarian to monitor the meeting and impose procedure using *Roberts Rules of Order*. The person running the meeting and the parliamentarian should not be the same person.

If you have trouble getting volunteers to attend regular meetings, here are some ways to add interest:

- Invite an outside speaker or performer. This can be anything from an hour-long presentation from an expert in your subject area to a five-minute story from a constituent your organization has helped.
- Include a hands-on or interactive activity. Ask participants to put fundraising ideas on index cards, create a problem-solving or team exercise, or even have attendees fold brochures during the meeting.
- Use audiovisual aids. Create a presentation using posterboard or a three-panel display to illustrate a recent activity or accomplishment, run photos on a screen, or show a video of your constituents.
- If the group is getting together for the first time, consider an ice-breaker activity.
- Children's activities can sometimes be fun for adults to revisit. Possibilities include Mad Libs, puzzles or trivia questions, scavenger hunts, and board games. These can be modified to incorporate information from the organization's area of interest.
- Offer food, even if it's just donuts and coffee or pizza. People sometimes enjoy potluck as a way of sharing foods they like.

QUESTIONS TO GET YOU STARTED

1. What steps could you take to minimize volunteers getting communications that don't pertain to them?
2. What tasks are you doing yourself that you might be able to delegate to someone else?
3. What systems might you put in place to ensure that volunteers are well matched to the tasks they are assigned?
4. What are some ways in which you could improve the effectiveness of your meetings?

CHAPTER 6

Policies, Procedures, and Liabilities

It is imperative that when thousands of selfless volunteers respond to those who have incurred the wrath of a natural disaster that legal liability need not be hanging over their heads.

—Jon Porter[1]

POLICIES

Written policies should clearly state what volunteers are permitted (and not permitted) to do. Unlike procedures, which tell volunteers *how* to perform tasks, policies tell volunteers *what* they can do. Policies clarify responsibilities and accountability, ensure continuity and uniformity, establish boundaries, define lines of communication, state organizational values and standards, and formalize the way an organization conducts its business and expects its volunteers to behave.

Some organizations have individual written policies, and others use a policy statement that covers all of their policies. A policy statement may also articulate the organization's philosophy or values.

If you question the need for formal policies and procedures, consider the story of the incredible shrinking gift shop from the *This American Life* radio show. It described the adventures of a young man who was made manager of the gift shop for a large arts center. The shop was staffed entirely by volunteers, most of whom were older adults. Initially, the new manager was charmed by the mom-and-pop atmosphere: no cash register (just a little cash box), volunteers that came and went whenever they wanted, even a stray cat that had taken up residence in the shop. But almost immediately, he realized that the revenues were far below what they should have been. In fact, nearly 40 percent of the sales weren't ending up in the bank. Profits were simply shrinking away. Was there a thief? The manager investigated but couldn't find an obvious culprit. So instead, he instituted policies and procedures that should have been in place all along: All purchases had to be recorded. Prices for all items were marked. Products were inventoried. Lo and behold, the shrinkage stopped. It turned out there had been dozens, perhaps even hundreds of thieves. Volunteers had come to view the gift shop as a sort of personal canteen. When they needed cab fare, they simply took it out of the cash box (they had, after all, just given several hours of their time, so a little compensation seemed fair). They picked up a tee shirt here and a toy for a grandchild there. Without rules and proper bookkeeping, the gift shop had become a free-for-all, with the organization funding the party. Instituting proper management, oversight, and financial cross checks solved the problem.[2]

Policies can't eliminate risk, but they can make sure that everyone is aware of potential risks and has been instructed on how to avoid them. Common topics for policies include:

- *Conflicts of interest.* Conflicts can arise when a volunteer is in a position to gain (money, a paying job, gifts, or special treatment) as a result of working for an organization. Potential conflicts do not have to disqualify volunteers but should be disclosed so that you can evaluate the likelihood of the conflict arising, determine how big a problem it would be, and counsel the volunteer about how to handle such situations.
- *Smoking, alcohol, weapons, and drugs.* This policy should cover both possession and use of these items, as well as any testing volunteers must undergo.
- *Affirmative action and diversity.* Affirmative action or inclusion statements are usually organization-wide policies, written by legal advisors, that cover paid staff as well as volunteers.
- *Abuse, sexual harassment and bullying.* This is another area in which the organization may already have policies that cover paid staff. Requirements for abuse clearances, background checks, and the process for handling complaints should be addressed.
- *Privacy and confidentiality.* This includes protection of health, financial, identifying, or other personal information of clients and volunteers, client confidentiality (information clients may disclose to volunteers),

and information the organization or agency does not want publicly disclosed.

- *Complaints and grievances.* Some organizations have whistle-blower policies that extend to volunteers. You should also have a system in place for how client and volunteer complaints and grievances are handled, including volunteer evaluation, discipline, and dismissal.
- *Use of vehicles (personal or organization-owned).* A policy is needed if volunteers drive clients or use vehicles as part of their volunteer activities. It should cover who is providing insurance, levels of authorization needed, and licensing, age, or other requirements for the driver.
- *Financial responsibility, money handling, and reimbursement.* This topic covers who is authorized to handle financial data and cash, how volunteers should handle any financial transactions, and reimbursement for travel or purchases.
- *Representing the organization.* This may be one or more polices that cover volunteers speaking to the media, committing the organization by signing contracts or liability releases, using their organizational affiliation in other settings such as employment or political work, and other limits on the volunteer's authority.

Writing good policies is somewhat of a special gift. Policies must be comprehensive yet still concise enough that people will read and understand them. They must be specific and clear, leaving no room for interpretation or misunderstanding. Here is an excerpt from the Purdue University volunteer policy statement:

> Purdue University is committed to providing a safe environment for work, study and outreach and to upholding the reputation and integrity of the University. To that end, all Volunteers will be subject to background screening that will include, at minimum, a Sex and Violent Offender Registry Check. Any individual listed on a registry that is part of the University's Sex and Violent Offender Registry Check or who has been convicted of an offense for which he or she must register as a sex or violent offender may not serve as a Volunteer.[3]

This statement is clear about the organization's philosophy, requirements, and standards.

Policies should be written in the present tense and should direct the reader in an authoritative manner. Include the positive (what is allowed) whenever possible. If appropriate, add illustrations or photographs to show the correct action or provide examples.

Policies are also a way to convey an organization's ethical, moral, religious, or philosophical positions. For example, here is part of a policy statement on political neutrality from The Church of Jesus Christ of Latter-Day Saints: "The Church's mission is to preach the gospel of Jesus Christ, not to elect politicians. The Church of Jesus Christ of Latter-day Saints is neutral in matters of party politics. This applies in all of the many nations in which it is established."[4]

Policies written by a committee are nearly always overly long, wordy, and convoluted, as each member of the committee feels the need to add a word here and a "what if" there. A better approach is to have the committee (usually comprising representatives from the paid staff, board, and volunteer management, as well as any legal and insurance advisors) provide a list of topics that should be addressed. This might include areas in which there is risk exposure, philosophies (values or beliefs) that should be articulated, rules that need to be clarified, and problem areas in which a change is needed in the way things are currently being done. Then, someone with good writing skills and a flair for concise wording should create a draft for approval. Any changes should pass the "is this really necessary?" test.

In terms of writing style, policies should have an imperative (command) tone to reinforce their importance: "Volunteers must have background checks and child abuse clearances on file before they have direct contact with children." They should be written in the active, not passive voice ("Volunteers must have ... " versus "It is required that ... "). Avoid words that provide wiggle room such as "nearly," "ideally," "should," "virtually," "suggested," and the like. Policies should contain the fewest words required to clearly state the policy.

Policies should be approved by the person who manages the volunteers, as well as the executive director, board, and any legal and insurance advisors. Having these groups involved in the development of the policies will help ensure their support when it comes time to implement the policies.

You may want to propose policies that are not currently in place but might improve the ways in which volunteers perform their tasks. You may observe these areas in the normal scheme of things, but you should make a point of questioning whether a policy is needed whenever there is a serious problem or consequence that was not covered by an existing policy.

Policies help protect against misunderstandings that might lead to unauthorized behavior or lawsuits, and for this reason you should have them reviewed by a legal advisor.

Before creating a new policy, you may want to search the Internet or ask similar organizations for copies of their policies on the topic. Chances are, something similar already exists. Starting with an existing statement will save time and help you make sure you haven't left any important points out.

PROCEDURES AND BEST PRACTICES

Procedures are the "how-tos" for the volunteer program. One place to start when creating written procedures is with industry best practices. Best practices are methods or techniques that have consistently provided results that are superior to those achieved through other means. They evolve over time as improvements are found and can be handed on to others to use as guidelines.

You can establish your own best practices, but by definition, best practices are those practices that have proven successful across a range of organizations. So a good place to start is by researching what other organizations or agencies are doing. Look for websites, online groups, Facebook pages, list-serves, and other resources that allow people to exchange ideas and develop best practices.

Some subject areas in which you may want to look for best practices include:

- Recruitment and selection of volunteers
- Orientation
- Training
- Meeting procedures
- Financial management
- Committees
- Risk management
- Communication (including use of social media)
- Retention
- Recognition
- Recordkeeping
- Evaluation

Another source of help is expert consultants or organizations that help nonprofits become more effective. A homeless services group turned to Volunteer Maryland, an organization that has worked with hundreds of nonprofits. The homeless services organization had been using volunteers throughout its 30-year history but recognized that it could be doing a better job managing them. Volunteers were coming in and doing a good job but were not coming back regularly; sometimes they would bring food for the shelter residents, but sometimes not, so the atmosphere was a little chaotic. Volunteer Maryland provided a trained coordinator who developed new procedures (including a calendar that told volunteers who was on duty along with when and what their assignments were) so that the volunteers and staff both knew what the volunteers were doing. This simple change made a huge difference. Volunteers provided food on designated nights, and the staff knew when they needed to provide food and when they didn't. The result was a savings of $2,000 a year in the food budget that they could then spend elsewhere.[5]

Written policies and procedures do not have to be lengthy and cumbersome. Maureen Eccleston says: "There are some organizations that have really intense policies and procedures for their volunteers, you know, 300 pages, and then there are other organizations that don't have any at all. Some organizations maybe just have a one-pager sort of a volunteer agreement, and our perspective is that any one of those is OK, as long as it works within your organizational structure." Eccleston advises looking at how you manage your paid staff. "If you have really intense policies and procedures for your staff members, then you probably want to have something fairly similar for your volunteers."[6]

LIABILITY

The issue of risk management and liability is extremely complex and in many cases requires the professional advice of insurance experts and lawyers. Laws vary country by country and state by state.

No matter how careful you are, accidents happen. And these days, that usually means someone gets sued. Fortunately, the Volunteer Protection Act of 1997 protects volunteers from liability for negligent acts or omissions committed while acting within the scope of their duties as volunteers.

This does not mean that volunteers are never liable for their actions. The act does not protect volunteers if their acts or omissions result from willful or criminal misconduct, gross negligence, reckless misconduct, or conscious or flagrant indifference to the rights or safety of the individual the volunteer harms. Nor does it cover volunteers if the harm is caused by the operation of a motor vehicle, vessel, aircraft, or other vehicle for which the state requires an operating license or insurance. Also, any misconduct that constitutes a crime of violence, a hate crime, a sexual offense, or violation of a federal or state civil rights law is not protected by the act. Finally, the volunteer is not protected if he or she was under the influence of alcohol or any drug at the time of misconduct.[7]

Make sure to check with your legal advisor to find out what is and isn't covered in your area. States can preempt the act if they have other laws that give volunteers additional liability protection. They can also choose to opt out of coverage under the federal law. States also can require organizations to provide mandatory training for volunteers, be liable for the acts or omissions of their volunteers to the same extent that they are liable for their paid staff, and/or carry insurance for individuals who may be harmed by volunteers.

Pfau Englund Nonprofit Law, P.C. suggests organizations limit their legal exposure by doing the following:

- Treat your volunteers like you treat your paid staff (develop volunteer position descriptions, use and carefully screen volunteer applications, and train and closely supervise your volunteers).
- Promptly investigate and respond to any complaints or concerns regarding a volunteer's actions.
- Secure insurance protection for your volunteers, as well as your staff, officers, and directors.[8]

The Nonprofits' Insurance Alliance of California and the Alliance of Nonprofits for Insurance classify nonprofit organization liability into three categories: direct liability, indirect or vicarious liability, and strict liability.[9] They define direct liability as when an organization or individual is held responsible for its actions or inactions. By this definition, an organization could be held directly liable for providing volunteers with unsafe equipment or sponsoring programs the group knows poses risks because they are not compliant with regulations. Not screening volunteers who work with children and not properly supervising volunteers also fall into this category.

They define indirect or vicarious liability as when an organization is held responsible for harm caused by persons acting on its behalf. Examples of indirect or vicarious liability include negligence on the part of a volunteer who damaged a parked car while leaving a parking space and medical expenses incurred by someone injured during an activity with a volunteer.

They define strict liability as when responsibility for harm is automatic and a finding of negligence or misconduct is not required, such as liability for a dog bite (in some states) and violations of some laws.

If the organization provides insurance, you should learn to what extent it protects you and the volunteers. You should also understand the risks the organization, the volunteers, and you yourself face, and then take whatever actions you can to minimize them.

One thing to consider is the seriousness of the risks the volunteer will be exposed to or expose others to. The higher the risk, the more carefully you should screen and train the volunteers. A volunteer that provides humanitarian assistance during a civil war is exposed to greater risk than a volunteer who provides blog content and works from home. Your oversight should reflect that.

Volunteers should be made aware of any unusual risks before they are selected and should be informed of any clearances, licenses, or permits that will be required. Volunteers should also be told specifically what they are and are not authorized to do, especially regarding activities that involve risk such as driving clients, working with children, and operating machinery.

Consult your insurance or legal professional before starting any new endeavors, and discuss liability concerns ahead of time with any companies, organizations, or individuals you collaborate with. For example, if you plan to run a house or garden tour as a fundraiser, will you be liable if someone falls? If you rent a facility, do you need contents insurance or liability coverage? If you plan to raffle off a car, is it insured while it is in your possession? You can get insurance riders to cover specific items or one-time events, but this must be planned for in advance. Increasingly, facility owners require liability waivers. Do not sign one until you have had the contract reviewed by a professional.

STANDARD OF CARE

A concept that often comes up in discussions of liability is "standard of care" or "duty of care." This refers to the organization's responsibility to provide a reasonable degree of care in protecting people from harm. In other words, did you take actions and maintain conditions that a reasonable person, following the standard practices of your industry, could assume would provide a safe environment? The standard varies from place to place and from situation to situation.

Some factors that would figure into a standard of care in a volunteer program include screening and training of volunteers, reference checks and background clearances, supervision of volunteers, implementation of industry best practices, and taking of precautions. The riskier the activity, the higher the standard of care required. The question to ask is "Have I done everything I can to protect my volunteers, clients, and the public?"

One place to look for standards is in similar organizations. Find out what procedures they are using, how they are training volunteers, what precautions they are taking, and so forth. You may also want to check with professional organizations for sample standards and practices. There is a lot of information available online. If you have a legal consultant or a volunteer lawyer in your organization, seek advice and clarification to make sure you have taken all the appropriate steps to address liability.

Finally, make sure your organization's legal and insurance consultants are fully informed of your activities, especially any that involve significant risks, and follow their advice in creating your policies and procedures. Don't assume that they understand everything you and the volunteers do.

RISK MANAGEMENT

Life is risky. Heck, getting out of bed is risky. You can't eliminate risk (unless you stay in bed, and perhaps not even then), but you can reduce risk, manage risk, and implement strategies to keep volunteers as safe as possible. This is not only your moral responsibility—in today's litigious world, it is also your legal and financial responsibility.

One way to assess risk is to look at who or what is at risk. There may be risks to the volunteers (from the public, use of machinery, exposure to disease), risks to the organization (theft, building damage, loss of reputation), and risks to the constituents or the public from the volunteers (injuries, sexual abuse, financial impacts from bad advice or misinformation).

Don't make the mistake of assuming that volunteers are not at any risk because they are never in risky situations. If you manage a needle-exchange program and volunteers are handling potentially infectious syringes, it is fairly easy to see some risk. On the other hand, if a volunteer is judging a flower show, the risk may be harder to see (until she gets bonked on the head by someone walking by carrying a wooden table, as happened to one of our Master Gardeners). Either way, risk exists and you need to do your best to minimize it and protect the volunteers.

Keep in mind that risks don't have to be physical. There can be risks from volunteers handling money or financial data, volunteers having access to clients' personal information, and volunteers damaging your organization's reputation. Your responsibility is to manage those risks, limit exposure to them, reduce the chances of a bad situation, and put procedures in place for dealing with problems when they occur. A fundamental principle of risk management when dealing with volunteers is "The more demanding the work, and/or the more direct the contact between the volunteer and the client, the greater the potential risk."[10]

Here are some questions to ask:

- What are the risks a volunteer might face?
- What are the risks specific to my organization or agency?
- Do volunteers understand the risks and know how they can minimize them?
- Are proper security precautions in place (identification badges, door locks, guards)?
- Is the facility safe (walkways clear, lighting present, parking area secure)?
- Are first aid materials and emergency equipment available and in good working order?
- Are there clearly written policies and procedures and do the volunteers follow them?
- Have volunteers been given adequate training?
- Are Material Safety Data Sheets (MSDS) and Occupational Safety and Health Administration (OSHA) information on hand for potentially dangerous materials or equipment?
- Are volunteers ever put in situations they aren't equipped to handle?
- Are precautions in place for dealing with allergies or other special issues volunteers or clients may have?
- Should vaccinations or health checks be required?
- Should drug tests be required?
- Should background checks or abuse clearances be required?
- Are volunteers expected to drive as part of their service? If so, does insurance cover them?

You also have a responsibility to protect the organization. This includes taking care of the organization's property, materials, and reputation, at least as far as the volunteer program is concerned. You can do this by minimizing conflicts of interest, properly training volunteers, having good policies and procedures in place, and identifying and remediating problems quickly and effectively.

You will also need to take steps to protect the organization's assets. If volunteers work with large sums of money, have access to high-value property, or handle credit card numbers, bank deposits, or other financial information, this is another potential risk that should be addressed.

Require background checks for anyone with direct access to cash or financial information. Institute cross-checks so that a single volunteer does not have exclusive responsibility for significant amounts of money. I extended this policy to include myself. When large amounts of cash came in at fundraisers, I insisted a staff member be present while the money was counted and put into the bank bag. This not only protected the organization, but also protected me from any accusations of wrongdoing.

You are also responsible for minimizing risks to the agency or organization's constituents. This includes protecting children and special populations from abuse, providing a safe environment whenever possible, and having policies and procedures in place so that volunteers don't exceed their authority (offer unauthorized medical advice, for example). Volunteers should be trained to use proper procedures to reduce risk wherever possible.

You may also want to have a crisis management plan. The plan can cover everything from protecting the safety of the staff and volunteers to the handling of media and public relations issues. For some organizations, a crisis management plan can be very simple. It might, for example, include procedures for evacuating the building, the chain of notification in case of an emergency, the location of first aid materials and emergency equipment, and procedures for securing the building. For organizations facing specific threats (such as a women's health clinic that provides abortions), a crisis management plan should be comprehensive and might even include periodic drills. Organizations with facilities located in dangerous areas, buildings subject to flooding or other problems, or clientele that can become violent or difficult to manage also fall into this category.

MANAGING RISK THROUGH TRAINING

Olympic swimmer Michael Phelps faced what could have been a catastrophe. Almost immediately after entering the water for the 200-meter butterfly final at the 2008 Olympics, his goggles filled with water and he couldn't see. Another swimmer might have stopped right there, but Phelps knew what to do because his coach often surprised him with unexpected obstacles to teach him to handle adversity and stay focused. In fact, the coach had once stepped on Phelps' goggles so that they would fill with water during a practice. In other words, Phelps had actually been *trained* to respond to this exact hazard. Phelps kept his cool and immediately began counting his strokes so that he would know when the turn was coming. He won the race.[11]

I'm not suggesting you intentionally step on volunteers' goggles or throw them into the deep end of the pool, but anticipating potential risks and addressing them during training is one way to minimize liability and help volunteers learn to remain calm when facing a potentially dangerous situation. For example, if volunteers are sometimes asked to help feed elderly residents of a nursing home, make sure they are trained what to do if a resident starts to choke. Role play and walk-throughs can be very memorable and build confidence. The proper response then becomes an instinctive reaction, and the volunteer is less likely to panic.

Volunteers working with potential hazards should be thoroughly briefed about what the hazards are and how to prevent injuries to themselves and others. Hazards include chemicals, body fluids, equipment and machinery (including specialized vehicles), medical materials, animals, and potentially dangerous people. Include discussions of personal safety, particularly if volunteers must work at night in dangerous areas or alone.

Training should also teach boundaries. There should be no misunderstanding regarding acceptable and unacceptable behavior, where the volunteer is permitted to go, what the volunteer is allowed to do, and what the limits of authority are for the volunteer. Directly address issues such as sexual harassment, bullying, and biased language and behavior in policy guides and during training. Some organizations also have policies that cover romantic relationships that present possible conflicts.

ABUSE CLEARANCES AND BACKGROUND CHECKS

Organizations have a responsibility to protect their paid staff, volunteers, and constituents. For that reason, you will need to screen potential volunteers for problems that could result in harm to other volunteers, staff members, or clients. While not foolproof, such screening tools can assist in identifying volunteers who have caused harm in the past.

Depending on the organization and the volunteer activities, in addition to employment and volunteer references, you may want to require credit checks, criminal background checks, child abuse clearances, sex offender checks, or other verifications. A search on the National Sex Offender Public Registry is a quick and cost-free step that can identify any applicants registered as sex offenders. The processes and fees for other kinds of screenings vary by state. Remember that it is a legal requirement to have an applicant's permission before conducting a criminal background check.

If the volunteer's work involves children or at-risk populations, you should require both a criminal background check and a child abuse clearance. You may also want to make some calls to references to confirm that there have been no reports of abusive behavior. This is an area in which it is impossible to be too careful. Even with such checks, you, staff members, and volunteers should be alert for any unusual behavior or problems. An abuse complaint should be dealt with immediately and reported to the authorities without hesitation. Just dismissing the volunteer or reporting the complaint to the director or board is not enough.

Some organizations require substance abuse tests. This can be an important consideration for volunteers who will have access to drugs or medical supplies, drive vehicles, operate machinery, work with children, or perform potentially dangerous tasks. If you plan to require such tests, it should be clearly stated in recruiting materials, applications, and during the interview process. You should also specify who pays for the tests and how often they will be required.

QUESTIONS TO GET YOU STARTED

1. Do you have policies in place to cover areas of risk and liability?
2. Are there tasks that could be made more efficient through written procedures?
3. Do you know whether insurance covers the volunteers?
4. What specific areas of risk can you identify within the volunteer program?
5. What changes could you make to your training program to further reduce risk?
6. What organizations or individuals might have best practices that would be useful?

CHAPTER 7

Special Kinds of Volunteers

Individual commitment to a group effort—that is what makes a team
work, a company work, a society work, a civilization work.

—Vince Lombardi[1]

TEAM VOLUNTEERS

Teams can be a particularly good arrangement for any tasks that lend
themselves to being performed by several people, such as staffing a booth
at a fair, registering and taking money for an event, or political canvassing. You might also consider team volunteers as a job-sharing strategy in
order to fill a difficult time slot or for splitting holiday duty.

Teams of two can be particularly effective. You can recruit two people
for the task initially or ask one person to find another volunteer to help.
"Bring a friend" volunteer opportunities can be a recruiting strategy for
short-term tasks and can bring new people into contact with the program.

Teams can consist of two evenly matched volunteers or an experienced
volunteer paired with a new worker. This is a good way for a new volunteer to get the hang of a complicated task in a nonthreatening, low-risk
way. For example, for a hotline, the new volunteer could observe and perhaps handle the paperwork or research required while the experienced
volunteer handles calls.

Teams can be particularly useful when two different types of skills
are required, such as an interviewer and a note-taker. Teams can help
provide security for tasks that involve visiting a private home or going

door-to-door. Teams also provide a social element that makes routine tasks more enjoyable. Even mundane tasks such as entering data or organizing an office can become fun when two people are sharing the assignment.

If you are assigning teams (rather than having people volunteer as a team), pay attention to personalities, skills, and ability to cooperate. Some people work well in this kind of situation, while others are better off on their own. Encourage the team to develop (within specified limits) its own approach to the task and its own work rhythm. For certain tasks, friendly competition among teams can add an element of fun and create a goal to work toward.

FAMILIES VOLUNTEERING TOGETHER

> Taking part in a positive volunteer experience with family members as a child increases one's likelihood of continuing to volunteer as an adult, which underscores the importance of promoting volunteering activities for children and families as well as adults.
>
> —Nadine Jalandoni and Keith Hume[2]

The number of people doing volunteer service with a family member is significant. During a survey on giving and volunteering in the United States, when people were asked, "Do you engage in volunteer activities with other members of your family?" 28 percent answered "yes."[3] Those who volunteered with family members tended to volunteer more often and exhibited a high level of commitment to the program.

Family volunteering also can increase volunteer satisfaction. "I do think that people enjoy it [volunteering] more if they are experiencing it with people that they know and people they'll go home to talk to about it,"[4] says Tia Milne, who works with family volunteers at the Northern Illinois Food Bank.

One way to encourage family volunteers is to offer activities that are appropriate for different age ranges. Activities such as putting in a garden, hosting an activity at a fair, or preparing a book sale can be structured for intergenerational teams. Clean-up days and other special events work well also.

You may need to be flexible about timing so that families can work around school and activity schedules. The increasing number of home-schoolers has created a new bank of potential volunteers who may be available during the day when children attending conventional schools are not.

For family volunteering to work, you have to recognize generational differences and be able to manage volunteers of different ages. Make sure staff members who will be working with family volunteers understand and like children. They should be patient and able to work with a variety of age groups. People with teaching backgrounds often make excellent coordinators for family volunteer groups. Provide training for the people who will supervise family volunteers so that they know what to expect, and emphasize the importance of having a thorough plan, especially when working with children.

Creating family-friendly volunteer opportunities takes a little effort but can have a very positive effect. According to a study by Independent Sector, family volunteers perform, on average, 23 percent more hours of volunteer work per week than other volunteers, and a higher proportion of them volunteer more frequently and on a more regular basis.[5]

You might start by simply inviting existing volunteers to bring one or more family members to a specific activity or event. This will help introduce them to the organization, allow them to see what their family member is doing, and give them the opportunity to make a contribution of their own. Even if they decide not to become involved, the family members will have a greater appreciation for the work the volunteer is doing and may be more supportive of the time being given to the volunteer program.

Volunteer Canada conducted a study that identified common characteristics of family volunteers. These included the perception that volunteering together provides a thread to connect various members of a family and the desire to engage teenage children in volunteering in order to instill values, shift attitudes of entitlement, and boost social awareness. The study also suggested that organizations consider virtual volunteer opportunities in which family members can participate using Skype or other online methods, casual or one-time opportunities to allow family volunteers to try out assignments, and opportunities that are perceived as family-friendly and enjoyable for all ages.[6]

Although you may find family volunteers have to work around a number of schedules and may have a harder time finding tasks that work well for intergenerational groups, these volunteers can be very energetic, enthusiastic, and effective. As with any volunteer activity, set clear expectations, provide guidelines, and match the task to the capabilities of the volunteers.

CORPORATE-SPONSORED VOLUNTEERS

> Corporate volunteering can be a low-cost, low-risk, high-impact way of gaining great resources and building strong relationships. Remember this is a win-win-win situation.
>
> —Lori Gotlieb[7]

Encouraging employees to volunteer is one way for companies to demonstrate their social responsibility and commitment to the community. Some companies have formal employee volunteer programs, while others support employee volunteers by providing a specified amount of paid leave for volunteer service.

Several kinds of volunteer assignments lend themselves to especially well to corporate volunteers:

- Board positions or professional service roles (lawyers, accountants, fundraising professionals, business leaders, bankers, etc.)
- Team challenges (groups of employees compete against each other in teams to collect donations, obtain sponsorships for walks or other events, develop special projects such as cleanup efforts, or provide mentoring services); clothing or food drives, charity tournaments, and sponsored walks or runs are good opportunities for team challenges.
- Corporate sponsorships (company volunteers participate in special events or fundraisers as a part of the company's financial sponsorship)
- Executives (or other trained professionals) on loan to nonprofit organizations
- Community projects (corporate volunteers help improve the neighborhood surrounding the company's facility by participating in beautification projects, painting and window washing, or community gardens)
- Corporations "adopting" an organization

Company-sponsored volunteers can be beneficial to all parties. Benefits to the employee include a sense of company pride, leadership and skill development, networking opportunities, and increased involvement in the community. Benefits to the company include improved morale, stronger employee commitment, and reduced turnover. Benefits to the organization include a new source of capable and committed volunteers, and a relationship with a company that might provide new insights, offer professional resources, and perhaps become a funding source. Companies may be more willing to help fund activities or provide other financial support for organizations in which their volunteers are working.

One caveat when working with companies: make sure the company doesn't have a hidden agenda, or you may find that the corporate volunteer comes with more strings than a marionette. Companies that have had a poor public image because of their products, their corporate policies, or the behavior of one or more of their executives, may want to use community service (and lots of self-generated publicity surrounding it) as a way of building goodwill. For example, companies that have poor environmental records often seek out environmental causes to support. This is called greenwashing because their real goal is to cover up their misdeeds and make the company appear environmentally responsible.

Organizations can get into trouble by partnering with a company that doesn't appear to be compatible with their mission. The Sierra Club took a lot of heat when it disclosed millions of dollars in donations from the fossil fuel industry.[8] And when the National Wildlife Federation teamed up with Scott's Miracle Gro, the Federation was flooded with comments on its blog and some people felt they had "sold their soul to the devil for a dollar."[9] Keep this in mind when choosing which companies to work with.

Another potential pitfall is the corporate volunteer day. Although on the surface it seems like a welcome prospect, Tia Milne explains the drawback: "They pick one day and want to save the world." A company might send out 150 employees on a single day for a designated number of hours. "In my opinion," says Milne, "I'd rather see less of that and more of the company actually embracing an organization and trying to work with them more long term and not as sporadically."[10] She advises developing a relationship with one or more companies so that the organization can explain what it needs, and together the organization and the company can develop a volunteer program that has real value.

If you don't already have a corporate partner, look first at companies in your immediate area. Start with the human resources or public relations office to inquire whether a formal program already exists that encourages employees to volunteer (time off, internal rewards, etc.). You may also want to ask whether management will list volunteer needs in company publications, on intranet sites or bulletin boards, or in a company email.

Building a relationship takes time but can have wide-reaching benefits. Invite a representative of the company for a tour or to attend a special event. If you have a volunteer already working for the company, ask for his or her help recruiting others from the company.

Look for projects the corporate volunteers can own. For example, if you run a food bank, you might approach a local company about creating a vegetable garden on its site that would be planted and maintained by its volunteers but provide vegetables for the food bank. An arts organization might approach a company about sponsoring a new event, with corporate volunteers selling tickets, seating people, helping set up and take down, and so forth.

If there is a specific company that would be a natural partner for your organization or agency, you may get more support. For example, a medical supply company would probably welcome a partnership with a health-related organization. A realty company might be interested in a project dealing with the homeless.

Lynn Spreadbury works with corporate partners who provide senior-level executives to Save the Children for three to six months at a time at remote locations such as Tanzania. Getting companies to make a commitment on that level takes time, but it gets back to making them real partners in the organization. "These are organizations that already partnered with us for years and years," Spreadbury explains. "They've probably been funding our programs, and now with this whole concept of getting your employees involved so they can really understand the corporation's philanthropic mission and understanding, now they're looking for opportunities for how they can engage their employees."[11]

UPS has taken corporate-sponsored volunteerism to new heights. UPS employees give an average of 80 hours of volunteer time each year. In 2010, that amounted to more than 1.2 million employee volunteer hours.[12]

Ronna Charles Branch, UPS Global Reputation Management PR Supervisor, explains that UPS considers itself a "doorstep company" because they deliver to doorsteps in communities across the country every day. They see UPS employees volunteering in those communities as just a natural extension of their work.

How can volunteer programs attract corporate volunteers like the ones at UPS? Branch says, "I think that it would be to the benefit of the organization to make it as convenient as possible for people to volunteer." She says organizations must also educate their volunteers about the difference they're making. "It's incumbent upon the organization to provide them [the volunteers] with an opportunity to use their skills and feel like they're making a difference. I think that's the reason why people volunteer." She adds, "The more personalized the message, the more people want to feel like there's a connection and they want to do their part to make it better."[13]

A study in Canada found that most corporate volunteers are looking for short-term, highly-skilled volunteer opportunities in organizations without rigid hierarchies and where volunteers are treated equally. Corporate volunteers like to measure their efforts and know that the impact they make is worth the time they're giving. Many want the ability to work off-site and don't want to waste time with an organization that isn't well structured and efficient. Despite the common one-day company volunteer events, most employees want a meaningful, longer-term volunteer engagement.[14]

COURT-ORDERED COMMUNITY SERVICE VOLUNTEERS

In the 1970s, judges began giving some convicted offenders an alternative to jail—they could serve their time by providing community service. To provide opportunities for these individuals, organizations are sometimes asked to take on one or more court-ordered community service volunteers. Most of these individuals are first-time offenders or have committed minor offenses, usually misdemeanors such as drug possession or driving infractions. Like any volunteers, some are unskilled and others have highly valuable skills.

The first thing to know about court-ordered (sometimes called court-mandated) volunteers is that you do not have to accept them if you don't want to. If you do, make sure your liability insurance will cover them. You must also take steps to ensure that you do not put volunteers, staff, clients, or the public at risk.

You should have specific policies that guide what types of offenders you are willing to accept, what tasks they will be allowed to perform, and what supervision they will require. For example, their service time will have to be carefully monitored and reported to the court. The volunteer time these individuals provide will be specified by the court, may be of longer duration than other volunteers (40 hours a week, for example), and will last for a specific period as well (six months, one year, two years). For this reason, you may have to construct the assignment around the volunteer instead of vice versa.

If you decide to accept court-ordered community service volunteers, be selective. For example, if your organization involves animals, you will not want to accept volunteers who have abused animals or exhibited violent behavior. If you are in a medical setting, you will probably not want volunteers who have had substance abuse issues. Groups that work with the public, such as public libraries, often will not accept volunteers who have committed sexual offenses, exhibited violent behavior, or had weapons charges. Do not put people in situations that could create problems for them or for you. For example, if you have a volunteer who has had a shoplifting charge, do not leave that volunteer alone in a setting that might be tempting.

Tia Milne uses court-ordered volunteers but raises the age requirement, tracks their hours more closely, and limits the number of volunteers per shift. Milne says, "We treat it as a separate program from our volunteer program, so they actually have to come in and they have to interview with a staff member and make sure they understand our guidelines."[15]

Although you are not required to accept court-ordered volunteers, remember that many bright and talented people make mistakes, especially when they are young. If your organization is willing to work with these individuals, you may be providing a turning point in someone's life and gaining a highly dedicated volunteer.

CHILDREN AND TEENS

There are a number of reasons you may want to include young people (perhaps even children) in your volunteer program. For starters, people who volunteer as children are more likely to volunteer when they are older. According to the Independent Sector, two-thirds of adult volunteers started volunteering as children.[16] According to the same study, those who volunteered when young and whose parents volunteered became the most generous adults in terms of giving time. And an additional bonus: people who volunteered as children were also more likely to donate money as adults.

Most young volunteers are in their teens or twenties. While volunteers in this age range may vary tremendously in maturity and skill level, a study in Canada found that youth volunteers (between the ages of 15 and 24) tended to be career-focused, flexible, and receptive to new ideas; more open-minded and accepting of diversity; energetic and enthusiastic; technologically savvy; and sensitive to perceived age discrimination. Although they may be volunteering to meet school community service requirements, they often see volunteering as part of their job search, skills development, and networking. They need flexible volunteer opportunities to accommodate commitments for school, work, friends, and family, and appreciate opportunities to receive constructive feedback and certification where possible.[17]

Organizations that actively cater to young volunteers will find it worth the effort. Jim Starr sees a growing number of young volunteers: "More and more young people want to be engaged in community service and volunteer efforts and so we've got a wide variety of efforts to help accommodate that."[18]

Ronna Charles Branch says: "The younger generation really likes getting involved and making a difference. They recruit more ... they want to talk to each other about it ... they want to get people more involved, and it's important to them that they work for a good organization . . . they're cheer-leaders for getting involved in the community."[19]

One way to accommodate their needs is to offer youth volunteers the kinds of opportunities they want. Meghan Kaskoun says, "Most of the young folks (and by that I mean 30 and under) who are coming in volun-teering want to just do a one-time opportunity. They want to see immedi-ate results. They want to come in and get some feedback immediately and see results from the work they're doing and it's mostly hands-on work."[20]

Tia Milne works with volunteers as young as eight, which presents spe-cial challenges. "They get so excited about working in the warehouse," she says, "that they may not pay attention to the guidelines."[21] Young children may also get bored or spend time talking with their friends, but they can be very energetic and enthusiastic helpers given some guidance and adult supervision. Milne's organization requires adult chaperones, whether it is one child or a group. The adult is expected to supervise the child so that staff time is not taken up babysitting.

Young volunteers perform best when expectations are kept high but rea-sonable. If you patronize, talk down, or overwork and underappreciate these energetic workers, you will not succeed. Adults tend to undervalue youth volunteers, expecting little and anticipating having to spend extra time getting them up to speed and supervising them to make sure they don't misbehave. With this sort of condescending attitude, it's no wonder their low expectations are met with poor performance.

Provide a secure environment for young volunteers in which any mis-takes are small ones, and any successes are easily recognized and rewarded. It is also best to keep volunteer tasks focused and limited in time (two-hour shifts, for example). Show that you welcome their opin-ions and efforts, respect them, and value their skills. Kaskoun recom-mends that when working with young people: "give them the space to learn and ask questions rather than assume they don't know what's hap-pening, and if they need some redirection, provide it."[22]

Provide youth volunteers with thorough and age-appropriate training, using hands-on opportunities (learning by doing) as much as possible. Keep in mind that their attention spans may be much shorter than you are used to. You may also find that some things you thought went without saying do not go without saying. For example, you may have to specify what does or does not constitute appropriate attire. You should also provide clear guidelines for cell phone use, as this can be a major distraction for young volunteers.

Make your expectations for service specific (time to report to work, length of shift, cancellation policy, and how much advance notice you need for schedule changes. Make it clear that you are depending on the volunteer because his or her contributions are a valued part of the operation. If you have volunteers who cannot hold to a schedule, try to create volunteer tasks (such as entering data or weeding a garden) that do not have to be done at a specific time. Find an arrangement that works well for both the volunteer and the program, and does not make the volunteer feel bad if other commitments prevent him or her from sticking to a schedule.

Jim Starr says, "One of the things that we're doing . . . is focusing on ways to get kids engaged in what we do as groups, because I think kids like to volunteer. One of the aspects that they enjoy is the social aspect—working with other kids in community service. So we are building activity guides that will engage a group of kids in our mission . . . These are easy-to-do projects or activities that can get them engaged in a one-time event that furthers our work."[23]

As with any volunteers, look for creative ways to use the skills and talents young volunteers offer. For example, many young people master technology easily. These volunteers may be able to assist with social media, help other volunteers learn computer skills, make improvements to the website, or even run virtual fundraisers or online auctions. Young adults and teens can also be great working with children and can serve as mentors, tutors, coaches, or teacher assistants.

Consider that youth volunteers—like adult volunteers—like to feel they are making a difference. Many young people are passionate about causes such as those involving the environment, human rights, animal protection, and child services. If you can channel this passion into volunteer activities that help advance the organization's mission, you will have happy volunteers and a more successful volunteer program.

Remember that young volunteers are fitting their service around other activities. For this reason, they may arrive hungry, so have some energy bars or small boxes of cereal and a water source available. If they are working through a mealtime, offer to provide pizza or sandwiches.

You will have to screen young volunteers as you would any volunteer, and you should make sure your organization won't have insurance or liability issues. Match skills, interests, and maturity level to the task.

Here are some categories of tasks that may work well for children and teens (with adult supervision):

- Building, painting, or assisting with maintenance tasks
- Visiting with seniors
- Assisting teachers

- Helping at food banks
- Gardening (especially growing food for food banks)
- Neighborhood beautification or community cleanup
- Working on environmental projects such as recycling, restoring habitat, or cleaning up beaches/streams
- Caring for animals
- Helping out at museums, libraries, or historic sites
- Working with political or activist organizations
- Fundraising (car washes, bake sales)

While young volunteers may not have as much time to give and may not be able to make long-term commitments, don't hesitate to include them in the volunteer program where possible. Like many adult volunteers, they may need to be asked, and you may have to explain where they can help.

INTERNS AND STUDENT VOLUNTEERS

The purpose of an internship is to get real-world experience through short-term supervised work as part of one's education. Most interns earn high school or college credit and some also receive a salary, although the pay is typically much lower than an employee would be given. Interns expect that their work will be a learning experience and possibly a path to paid work and a career. Sometimes that is the case; other times interns perform menial work and get little real experience.

Unlike most volunteers, interns often work for for-profit companies. According to the National Association of Colleges and Employers "2012 Internship & Co-op Survey" report, employers plan to increase internship hires by 8.5 percent over last year, and nearly all of those answering the survey expect to pay their interns.[24] However, no statistics are kept on the number of interns who work for profit-making companies without pay, and other sources claim unpaid internships are common, even though they are often in violation of the Fair Labor Standards Act.[25] According to an article published in the *New York Times*, some experts estimate that one-fourth to one-half of student internships are unpaid.[26]

Some interns do not even receive academic credit. A recent Intern Bridge survey of more than 42,000 students nationwide found that 18 percent of interns do not receive monetary compensation or college credit. If true, that would be a major violation of the Fair Labor Standards Act.[27]

Some experts complain that companies and organizations use unpaid internships to avoid having to pay and insure an employee and that they use interns to perform menial tasks that have little educational value. Unpaid internships also create inequality because only those students who can afford to work for free can take advantage of them. Some colleges are responding to the growth of unpaid internships among for-profit organizations by not offering academic credit for unpaid internships.

According to the Fair Labor Standards Act, if all of the following criteria apply, the students are not employees within the meaning of the act:

1. The training, even though it includes actual operation of the facilities of the employer, is similar to that which would be given in a vocational school.

2. The training is for the benefit of the trainees or students.

3. The trainees or students do not displace regular employees but work under close supervision.

4. The employer that provides the training receives no immediate advantage from the activities of the trainees or students, and, on occasion, the employer's operations may even be impeded.

5. The trainees or students are not necessarily entitled to a paying job at the conclusion of the training period.

6. The employer and the trainees or students understand that the trainees or students are not entitled to wages for the time spent in training.[28]

Note that according to requirement 4, the intern should be of no help, and may actually be an impediment to the company that employs him or her. For this reason, companies and organizations should be careful when structuring positions for unpaid interns.

If structured properly, internships can provide a benefit for both the employer and the student. For example, offering internships to underprivileged students as a way of teaching job skills and providing them an entry to the paid workforce can be a way to provide opportunities and create goodwill in your community.

In the nonprofit world, according to Susan Ellis, "The differences between interns and other volunteers relate mainly to what assignments may be given to each and which staff members should supervise them."[29] Interns, if working for college credit, may have to be supervised by a particular person or in a particular way, and there may be specific hours or additional paperwork required in order for the volunteer to receive credit. Some organizations classify internship jobs differently from volunteer jobs. Ellis thinks it is unfair for nonprofits to create challenging, intensive positions for interns and not offer these opportunities to any volunteers who meet the requirements.

As with other volunteers, you should have a plan in place before you accept interns. Internships can be a good way of getting skilled volunteers, but even nonprofit organizations must respect the goal of the internship, which is to teach the student, not benefit the organization.

Another type of student volunteer you might be offered is a work team provided by a university business school or a fellow provided by an organization such as AmeriCorps. Business educators often look for real-world opportunities for their students and invite local businesses and nonprofit organizations to participate. Projects they offer may include helping you with your strategic plan, developing (and possibly implementing) a project, or conducting a business analysis of your organization. These projects generally are conceived, developed, and completed within a single school semester.

Business school projects, like internships, are designed to benefit the students. The students may or may not have any interest in or expertise with nonprofit businesses. For this reason, you should consider such opportunities as good deeds that will take some staff or volunteer time and which may or may not provide value to the organization.

Fellowships provide students (generally seniors or graduate students) stipends while they perform their service. Like the work teams, the benefits of fellowship programs vary, based on the skills of the student.

OLDER VOLUNTEERS

> Baby boomers—the generation of 77 million Americans born between 1946 and 1964—represent a potential boost to the volunteer world, not only because of the sheer size of the generation but also because of its members' high levels of education, wealth, and skills.
>
> —Corporation for National and Community Service[30]

The baby boomer generation is not only large, but also has the highest rate of volunteerism of any age group.[31] The more hours a baby boomer devotes to volunteering, the more likely it is that he or she will volunteer from year to year.[32] Nearly eight out of 10 baby boomer volunteers who serve 100 to 499 hours a year volunteer again the following year, compared to just over five in 10 who serve one to 14 hours. Some are retired, but even those who aren't are often working paying jobs with reduced demand, fewer hours, or both.

A study in Canada found that boomer volunteers had exceptionally high participation rates and volunteered more hours, on average, than other groups. They want organizations to be efficient and effective in their management of volunteers and staff, and want to see the impact they are making. They like activities that offer a chance to act outside their skill and knowledge base and do things that are different from their daily work. Boomers like working independently and are willing to stay at an organization for many years as long as they are treated well.[33]

Meghan Kaskoun notices that her organization is getting more baby boomer volunteers, and like a lot of other volunteers, they don't want to just do menial work. She says organizations are being challenged to develop "enticing positions, stimulating positions, to challenge baby boomers who came in and, they used to run organizations and now they are wanting to be challenged at that kind of level, utilize some of their skills and help an organization so people are having to create positions or modify what they're already doing."[34]

Boomers have lifelong connections, networking skills, life experience, and enthusiasm. If you can engage baby boomer volunteers as collaborators in achieving the goals of the organization or agency, you may be able to leverage a tremendous source of talent and energy that will have a multiplier effect through their influence in the community and access to financial resources.

As people reach their 60s, they may begin shifting their emphasis from financial rewards to personal fulfillment. For this reason, aging baby boomers and seniors are prime candidates for volunteer recruitment.

Seniors (people over 65) are healthier and more active than they ever have been before. They often have valuable skills, work experience, and street smarts that can come in very handy. These older adults may make excellent board candidates or members of an advisory group because of their life and job experience. A retired business executive, for example, may be able to help you with strategic planning or running meetings smoothly, while a volunteer who was once a teacher might do very well working with children or assisting with your training program.

Older adults may be free to travel for overseas programs and be better able to attend meetings or engage in activities during traditional working hours. They may be happy to contact people by phone, a time-consuming task that many younger people resist, yet for an older person with plenty of time, it represents an opportunity to be sociable and make an impact. Seniors often have skills younger people never learned such as sewing, minor carpentry, plumbing, and auto repair, and they probably have better handwriting for addressing invitations or filling out certificates.

According to a report by the Urban Institute, it is important to engage older adults in volunteer activities early on, ideally before they retire, because this improves the odds of them volunteering in later years. The Institute looked at volunteer activities by adults age 55 to 65 between 1996 and 2004 and found that nearly seven of eight older adults who volunteered in 1996 volunteered again by 2004, and nearly four in 10 volunteered consistently over the eight-year period. Only about a third of those who did not volunteer in 1996 did any volunteering by 2004.[35] This indicates that the way to engage the highest number of older adult volunteers is to get them involved *before* they become seniors.

One challenge with senior volunteers is dealing with what to do when they can no longer do tasks safely. Meghan Kaskoun had this problem. "A lot of folks were getting older and couldn't move up and down the steps or lead an evacuation as quickly as was necessary. We actually walked them through that process as if it was an evacuation and a lot of folks realized that they just weren't physically able to do it and made the decision themselves not to continue even though they were enjoying it. They just realized that they weren't able to meet our needs even though we were meeting theirs."[36] In these cases, reassignment can save face for the volunteer and prevent possible injury. The volunteer may be able to be placed in a training or advisory position, supervising other volunteers. Or if the volunteer is unable to work at all, a good solution may be to create an "emeritus" status that allows them to stay involved with the organization.

You may need to be particularly alert for generational differences if you are a young manager working with older volunteers. For example, you may need to consciously slow down your speech and speak louder (particularly if your voice is high-pitched) when speaking with older volunteers. Sometimes it is hard for an older person to resist sharing their decades of knowledge. It will do both of you good if you give this input a sincere listen. Older volunteers may or may not have useful suggestions, but you have to handle their contributions gracefully, while drawing the line at your decision-making authority.

Older adults vary in how well they've kept up with technology. Do not assume that an older volunteer will not be able to use computer databases, online tools, mobile apps, cloud-based programs, or other kinds of technology. But also don't assume a short learning curve. Some older people get overwhelmed quickly when it comes to new gadgets. And even those older adults who use computers routinely may not be familiar with the ins and outs of social media and smartphones.

You may also find that older adults check email less frequently and may not use instant messaging or Facebook. Older people may also be less likely to keep political opinions to themselves and may be less comfortable with diverse audiences, which may necessitate a counseling session. On the plus side, older volunteers generally bring valuable experience and life skills, value hard work, and can be extremely loyal and dependable once they become a part of the organization.

Look for ways to engage even the oldest volunteers by offering opportunities that do not rely on physical endurance or speed. Tasks such as mentoring, greeting, baby cuddling, and serving as a companion are just a few of the roles an older volunteer might play.

As with all volunteers, an important key to recruiting older adults is to ask. According to an Independent Sector survey, if asked, 84 percent of seniors volunteered; if not asked, only 17.4 percent did so.[37] Yet according to the same survey, less than one-third of all seniors over age 65 were asked to volunteer. By providing opportunities for older volunteers, asking them to become involved, and showing that their contributions will have tangible results, you will benefit from this vast and growing source of volunteers.

PEOPLE WITH DISABILITIES

People with disabilities have historically been seen as recipients of volunteering (clients) rather than people who have skills of value to volunteer-involving organizations. Misconceptions about the numbers, interests, and capabilities of these individuals have kept organizations and agencies from fully engaging an enormous number of potential volunteers.

According to the U.S. Census Bureau, approximately 56.7 million people (nearly 19 percent) of the civilian noninstitutionalized population had a disability in 2010.[38] Few groups have a volunteer workforce that reflects numbers anywhere close to that percentage.

Inclusion takes a little effort. It starts with making sure your recruitment information is available in multiple formats and can be accessed in a variety of ways. Offer help in filling out application forms or other paperwork. Make your facility as accessible as possible. When you recruit, reach out to local disability support organizations and advertise in publications targeted to people with disabilities.

There is a huge spectrum of abilities and disabilities, so if you manage a group of volunteers, it is nearly certain that you are already working with people who have limitations of one kind or another. Yet by providing an accessible workplace, a variety of volunteer tasks, appropriate training, inclusive methods of communication, and an attitude that supports equal opportunity, you may be able to attract a more diverse group of volunteers.

Disabilities such as sight or hearing impairments, mobility or strength restrictions, or cognitive disabilities can be addressed on an individual basis by evaluating the person's skills and abilities against the tasks available, just as you would for any volunteer. It will help if you focus on their capabilities rather than their disabilities.

Learning disabilities, attention deficit syndrome, autism spectrum disorder, and other, less visible, impairments can be more difficult to discern, but must also be addressed in order to make a good match between the volunteer and the assignment. Someone who cannot process language easily, for example, may make an excellent technology assistant; while a person with poor interaction skills might be very good at organizing a database or physical space such as a publications room.

Accommodate volunteers with special needs in a way that does not single them out. If you have a volunteer with a hearing impairment (with volunteers over the age of 60, this is almost a given), use a microphone for large meetings or noisy settings and make sure you also provide the information in written form if possible. If you have volunteers with vision impairments, remember to keep type size large on all your documents and communications, and use a large screen and large type for PowerPoint presentations. Also make sure the floors and corridors are kept free of debris, cords, or other items that someone with imperfect vision might trip over.

Identify tasks that could be performed by someone with limited mobility. Assignments that can be completed online, phone work, and tasks that can be completed at home are just some of the options. Offer flexible positions and tasks with flexible deadlines.

Treat volunteers who have disabilities with respect and courtesy, and match them to the appropriate positions as you would any volunteer. Make sure that all volunteers understand the organization's commitment to inclusion and do not tolerate signs of disrespect or lack of cooperation. Remember that volunteers with disabilities—like other volunteers—want to learn new skills, meet new people, build self-confidence, and make a difference in the world.

"VIRTUAL" VOLUNTEERS

One of the growing areas of volunteerism developed out of the need to accommodate increasingly crowded schedules, combined with the availability of new communication technology. "Virtual" volunteers are volunteers you will not work with face-to-face, and in fact may never see, but who will perform their tasks from somewhere other than your site, perhaps from another state or country. Managing volunteers who are not physically present creates unique challenges.

You may find it harder to bond with, supervise, and reward virtual volunteers. The volunteers themselves may feel unsupervised, which can lead to more innovation (on the positive side) and less adherence to policies and procedures (on the negative side). There will also be a lack of camaraderie within the volunteer group, although this can be dealt with to some extent through conference calls, web-based collaboration tools, or occasional face-to-face meetings. On the positive side, you have an almost limitless source of volunteers and a greatly increased variety of skill sets and capabilities.

Tasks that are suited to virtual volunteers vary. Virtual assignments can be performed by someone nearby or on the other side of the globe (or by people with disabilities that make traveling to your site difficult). Assignments can be short term, but do not have to be and you may well want to develop long-term relationships with good virtual volunteers.

Websites such as VolunteerMatch and Craigslist are well suited for listing virtual volunteer positions. You will need to train and supervise virtual volunteers, and review their work as you would any volunteer.

MICROVOLUNTEERING AND CROWDSOURCING

A relatively new style of volunteering—microvolunteering—has developed as a way to address the fact that many people have the motivation to volunteer but lack large blocks of time. Koodonation, an online microvolunteering community, uses these four characteristics to define microvolunteering:

- *Convenient.* It's volunteerism that fits into your schedule when you have free time. The tasks are simple, so there is usually no training or vetting required. And it's all done online so that you can volunteer from anytime anywhere—even your couch!
- *Bite-sized.* There's a reason they call it microvolunteering. Volunteer tasks are broken into small-ish pieces, so they're quick and easy to

solve. So if you only have a little time to help/spare, you can still make a big difference.

- *Crowdsourced.* Crowdsourcing means that anyone and everyone can help. And when it comes to coming up with ideas to help nonprofits and solve challenges, a crowd of heads is better than one!

- *Network managed.* As microvolunteers post all of their ideas and responses, the community provides added value in rating the responses and helping nonprofits decide which solutions are best. So even your opinion can help.[39]

At Koodonation (and other sites such as Sparked.com and HelpFrom Home.org), nonprofit organizations list "challenges," which are specific, well-defined, low-commitment (often taking 30 minutes or less) projects that can be done completely off-site (usually online) by volunteers. Volunteers select causes that interest them and indicate what skills they can offer. Volunteers are then matched to appropriate challenges and can respond to the ones that interest them.

Crowdsourcing is used in the for-profit world to outsource problems or projects to anyone who wishes to work on them. Problems may be small as with microvolunteering challenges, but don't have to be. Participants propose solutions, and the company provides feedback. The company pays for any solutions it accepts. Nonprofits can also take advantage of crowdsourcing, either to obtain low-cost services or to obtain volunteer participation.

The biggest difference between traditional volunteer assignments and microvolunteer or crowdsourcing challenges is that one challenge may result in many responses. If, for example, you post a challenge to develop a new logo, instead of recruiting a single volunteer, you may get a number of responders who take up the challenge. They will post their responses, which site visitors can critique. You can review the selections (and the comments) and provide feedback, which will generate another round of responses. Through this collaborative process, you arrive at a logo you accept and the challenge is closed.

Microvolunteering is developing its own culture and etiquette. Volunteers can track their time and get ratings; organizations can give awards and provide visibility for successful projects. This creates a sense of community and adds a social networking component.

You may also want to try Twitter or Facebook as a way of reaching potential volunteers with microvolunteering or crowdsourcing opportunities. Some organizations are using phone apps (either their own or one such as VolunteerMatch) for microvolunteering opportunities as well. You can use these tools in a similar way to invite volunteers to propose the solution to a problem, participate in a project, or complete a task.

Microvolunteering and crowdsourcing opportunities are perfect for people with disabilities or those who are housebound, volunteers who prefer to work alone, people who don't live near organizations they want to assist, volunteers who don't want to make a large commitment, people who have only small amounts of free time (or time available only in small blocks), and people who want to make a difference in a lot of different ways or for many different organizations.

VOLUNTOURISM

Volunteer tourism, or "voluntourism," is when people spend vacation time doing work for no pay, generally for a cause they support or in a geographic area that needs help.[40] While missionaries have been doing this for a long time, the tourism industry has now jumped aboard, and like ecotourism, voluntourism has become a growth market. Some standard tours have added a volunteer opportunity during the trip, while others design vacations around volunteerism. There are now even websites that offer honeymoon volunteer packages ("honeyteering").

In 2007, 3.7 million people reported doing volunteer work at least 120 miles from their home.[41] Volunteers travel to historically needy locations in Africa and other regions, or go to areas following disasters like Hurricane Sandy to do what they can. Jim Starr deals with this all the time: "We see that come up when we have these large catastrophic disasters when people feel this need to help and they'll take their vacation time and want to go help."[42]

For years, Road Scholar (previously Elderhostel) has offered service learning opportunities in which people essentially pay for the opportunity to volunteer at a wide variety of sites around the world. Participants take part in projects such as helping Yellowstone National Park archive its history, tracking humpback whales in Costa Rica, or teaching English in Italy. In some cases, part of the cost of these programs may be tax deductible.

In some areas, nonprofit organizations have taken advantage of volunteer tourists coming to them. CAMP Rehoboth, an organization that fosters inclusivity and supports the lesbian, gay, transgender, and bisexual community in the resort town of Rehoboth Beach, Delaware, offers a Volunteers on Vacation program for people who want to devote time to helping plant gardens in subsidized housing communities, working with children, or helping with other community service projects while they are vacationing in the area.

QUESTIONS TO GET YOU STARTED

1. What special types of volunteers are you not working with that you might?
2. Do any volunteer assignments lend themselves to team, corporate, or family groups?
3. Are there ways you might create more challenging assignments for motivated volunteers?
4. Are you providing opportunities for volunteers with disabilities?
5. Are there any tasks that could be performed by "virtual" volunteers or posted on microvolunteering or crowdsourcing sites?
6. Are you located in an area that attracts tourists who might be encouraged to volunteer while they are in town?

CHAPTER 8

Retention, Recognition, and Rewards

Next to physical survival, the greatest need of a human being is psychological survival, to be understood, to be affirmed, to be validated, to be appreciated.

—Steven Covey[1]

WHY VOLUNTEERS LEAVE

A first step toward learning how to keep volunteers is to understand why volunteers leave. There are some general reasons volunteers leave (poor task/volunteer match, volunteer's time is being wasted, volunteer didn't feel appreciated), there may be reasons specific to the organization (inefficient structure, personality issue, change in mission), and there may be personal factors you cannot control (family pressures, work demands, health issues).

Here are the most common reasons volunteers give for leaving an organization:

- Poor match between skills/interests and tasks
- Too much bureaucracy
- Feeling "used"
- Politics/personality conflicts
- Inadequate support
- Dissatisfaction with the way the organization is run

- Change in the organization's mission or direction
- Little or no chance for personal development or growth
- Unclear goals or expectations
- Lack of praise, rewards, or recognition
- Feelings of being powerless to make a difference in the organization
- Tasks are too mundane or boring
- Lack of support
- Lack of prestige
- Lack of opportunities to demonstrate initiative and creativity

An exit interview is a good way to show volunteers you valued their service and may give you some insight into why they decided to leave; however, most people will not be fully candid with the interviewer, particularly if that interviewer is the person in charge of the volunteers. A better approach is having a neutral party (perhaps another volunteer or someone from another part of the organization) conduct the interview. This should not be a board member or officer because that can also be intimidating. The interview should be done either on the phone or somewhere the volunteer will be comfortable.

Another approach is an exit survey (mailed or online). Ideally, the exit survey should be conducted at a specific time of year so that you can survey as a group any volunteers who have left during the year and therefore make the survey anonymous.

Observe when volunteers tend to leave your organization. This may provide clues about why they are leaving and help you identify problem areas. Studies have indicated that for most organizations, the first six months is critical to volunteer retention.[2] It is during this initial period that the volunteer gets to know the people, the organization, and the assignment, so in some cases, lack of retention comes when expectations aren't met.

You can reduce early dropouts through careful screening, orientation, and training. Make sure your selection process is screening out volunteers who are not well matched to the organization or the position. Make sure the training program is giving volunteers the knowledge and skills they need, along with the confidence to work effectively. Monitor new volunteers carefully to make sure their expectations are reasonable and are being met, and that they understand their responsibilities and are performing well.

If you can increase volunteers' commitment level by improving the bond between volunteers and the organization, they will be less likely to leave. Commitment level is significantly greater when volunteers are strongly supportive of the organization's mission and feel a part of it. You can also increase commitment by fostering teamwork (which increases interpersonal bonds), involving other family members (which also improves bonding), and developing a tiered system of rewards or recognition (the longer volunteers stay, the greater the rewards), adding benefits, or offering preferred status connected with longevity.

You should also periodically check even long-term volunteers to determine their level of satisfaction with their role. People who have been doing the same task for a long time may want to try something new or may need a fresh challenge. People's lives and schedules change as well, and by accommodating these changes, you may be able to avert the loss of an experienced volunteer.

Unfortunately, many people will not express their feelings (or will not express their feelings strongly enough) until they have already made the decision to leave. Fear of confrontation or of letting the organization (or the manager) down can reduce the volunteer's willingness to indicate dissatisfaction. Unless you maintain open communication and probe to get honest feedback, you may not know that a volunteer is unhappy until he or she departs.

The end of a project, service term, or major activity is a point at which you can lose volunteers. Lynn Spreadbury works with volunteers who spend weeks or months at a time at a service location and then go home. Her challenge is keeping volunteers engaged with the organization. "Towards the end of the volunteer opportunity we put together information on how the participants can stay involved with the organization," she says. "A lot of times what happens is you go on a service trip and it's a really powerful, moving experience and then you come back home and there's often a disconnect ... what we try to do is create a little bit of an alumni community, where people that have done service trips can all stay together and they keep that spirit alive." She makes sure they are invited to local fundraising events and nearby activities, and keeps the lines of communication open. "So we try to make it a little more holistic rather than just that one-time experience."[3]

Some types of volunteers have specific needs and therefore require different techniques for improving retention. For example, studies show the key to retaining baby boomer volunteers is establishing an ongoing commitment that is intellectually challenging. The year-to-year retention rate for baby boomer volunteers who perform more challenging assignments such as professional or management activities (like strategic planning, volunteer management and coordination, and marketing) is 74.8 percent, followed by baby boomers who engage in music or other performance arts

(70.9 percent), and those who do tutoring, mentoring, and coaching (70.3 percent).[4]

A Canadian study found that the optimal formula to engage volunteers strikes a balance between:

- Designing specific, set roles and being open to volunteers determining the scope of what they can offer
- Being well organized but not too bureaucratic
- Matching skills to the needs of the organization but not assuming that everyone wants to use the skills related to their profession, trade, or education[5]

EMPOWERMENT

The best executive is the one who has sense enough to pick good men to do what he wants done, and self-restraint enough to keep from meddling with them while they do it.

—Theodore Roosevelt[6]

Whether you call it "taking ownership," "buying-in," or "empowerment," the truth is that people work harder for something they own. If volunteers feel as if they are working for you, they may do a decent job; if they feel they are working for the organization, they will do a better job; if they feel they are working for *their* organization, they may do a phenomenal job. This goes beyond teamwork, although that is part of it. If you create an environment in which volunteers' ideas are not only accepted, but also encouraged, recognized, and rewarded, you will find volunteers will participate more enthusiastically.

Encouraging volunteer decision making can be done in various ways. For a new project or activity, you might have a brainstorming session and be open to ideas, writing them all down without critique or comment. Then after everyone who wants to has contributed, you can (as a group) begin to eliminate ideas that don't fit the mission, are too costly, or are otherwise impractical. Then you can group similar ideas, combine suggestions that seem to work well together, and eventually settle on a group-created concept.

Another way to provide autonomy is to establish some basic ground rules and then let the volunteers take it from there. You may be surprised to find that volunteers often come up with ways of doing things that are much different from your own but still completely acceptable and highly successful.

This is particularly true with strategies for organizing the functions a volunteer has experience with. For example, you may have a volunteer who works on a hotline. You need to capture certain information about the callers but can be flexible about how that is done. If you allow the volunteer to propose some possible solutions, you may end up with an online database, a fill-in-the-blank entry form, or a grid-style workbook. If you need a paperless solution, specify that and the volunteer may come up with an Excel format, an online database, or a cloud-based solution. The organization gets what it needs, and the volunteer has the sense of pride that comes with ownership.

Considering volunteers a part of the staff rather than just support for the staff can make a big difference in the attitudes of the volunteers and everyone else in the organization. The American Red Cross treats its volunteers as if they were employees. "Our volunteers are empowered to make operational decisions within the parameters and guidelines that we set for our disaster relief operation," says Jim Starr. "A volunteer goes through the same basic orientation that an employee does, so they're provided the same kind of overview of the organization in orientation. We have a volunteer handbook that is very similar to our employee handbook in terms of what is expected of an employee, how to work within the organization, and [things of] that nature. They are trained . . . they have the ability to move up into management and supervisory positions . . . volunteers are provided for the most part with access to our internal communications . . . so they're provided a lot of the same kind of information that an employee would be as well."[7]

One thing that helps empower volunteers is good organization. Providing a structure, within which the volunteer is free to operate, allows the volunteer to comfortably make decisions and choose how a project or task is implemented.

Cynthia Myers, Facilitator of the Family Council at Ingleside at King Farm in Rockville, Maryland, wanted to provide volunteers (who visit residents at assisted living facilities) with the tools they needed to be effective. She started by developing tip sheets on topics such as talking with older people, working with people with hearing impairments, and starting conversations with people with short-term memory loss. Sometimes, volunteers didn't know what to do with the residents, so Myers created an accordion file with instructions for games that were available at the facility. Descriptions and instructions for each game went into a separate section of the folder. Volunteers coming in to work with the residents could thumb through the file and find a game that fit the time available and the capabilities of the resident. This gave the volunteers plenty of leeway in making their own choices, while saving them time and giving them ideas for activities that had proven successful in the past.[8] A similar idea file could be created for dog walkers (maps of good routes, favorite toys or games), volunteers working with children (age-appropriate activities), hospital visitors (inexpensive or free items appreciated by patients), fundraising committees (themes and event concepts), shelters and clinics (books to read to children, good waiting room activities), and political workers (walk routes, call lists, phone scripts).

SENSE OF BELONGING

One of the most powerful motivators is a sense of belonging (it is one of the needs Abraham Maslow described in his famous theory on the hierarchy of needs[9]). Creating team spirit, shared vision, and a sense of community is one of the best things you can do for an organization.

Some ways to build a sense of community include:

- A common goal
- A common enemy (for organizations working toward curing a disease, for example)
- Shared values
- Shared responsibility
- Cooperative idea generation/solution formulation
- Respect for and support of each other
- A feeling of synergy from the use of volunteers' individual strengths to create a better effort overall

Jason Zigmont uses the sense of belonging as a retention tool for members of a fire department (who are volunteers). "Once the member has gone inactive," Zigmont says, "the best way to bring them back is to keep them involved and informed. This means inviting them to all of the social events and making a special call to them from time to time. The key is to let the member know they are still welcome and the department will be there when they are ready to come back."[10]

Don't overlook the role of the family when it comes to volunteering. A study of older volunteers found that volunteers who contribute intensely and for many years and who are married to volunteers are the least likely to quit. And nonvolunteers are more likely to take the leap if they have been uninvolved for a few years and their spouses volunteer.[11]

A sense of belonging is sometimes the prime motivator for a volunteer. People who are single or have lost a spouse, those who've had children grow up and move away, and people who are retired or who have become unemployed may long for that sense of connectedness that makes people feel needed. They themselves may not even recognize how essential the sense of belonging is to their motivations for volunteering. Creating a welcoming volunteer community will lead to happier, healthier volunteers who will stay with the organization longer.

While a sense of belonging is a powerful motivator, be careful not to create such a sense of inclusiveness that the group becomes a clique. Talk to the group about welcoming new volunteers. Pair new recruits with experienced volunteers on team projects or in mentoring programs and help bring them into the group smoothly.

PERSONAL GROWTH

One of the rewarding things about working with volunteers is having the opportunity to help them with their own development. It is a great feeling to help someone become a better person. Personal growth is one of the reasons people volunteer and even if it isn't a specific goal, volunteers who gain new skills have a sense of reward that makes them more inclined to stay with the organization.

You can enhance the opportunities volunteers have for self-improvement in the following ways:

- Offer advanced training or certification options.
- Encourage volunteers to learn new skills.
- Encourage volunteers to confront fears (to try public speaking, for example).
- Provide levels of advancement within the volunteer ranks to give volunteers a chance to experience leadership.
- Expose volunteers to aspects of the organization beyond their particular volunteer task.
- Allow volunteers to shadow or work alongside paid staff.
- Encourage volunteers to take advantage of external training opportunities.
- Notice and encourage aptitude. For example, if someone shows signs of creativity, give that individual a project that allows for creative interpretation.
- Have high expectations for volunteers and encourage them to have high expectations for themselves.

- After the successful completion of an activity or project, provide the opportunity for greater responsibility.
- Give experienced volunteers the opportunity to mentor and encourage others.
- Periodically evaluate volunteers and ask them where they see themselves going and what new opportunities they would like to have.
- Be a good coach and cheerleader. Give credit where credit is due, publicize volunteer successes, show lots of appreciation, and keep encouraging volunteers forward.

SOCIALIZING

Another reason many people volunteer is to meet people. Socializing can be very energizing for volunteers, and can help encourage new ideas and fresh viewpoints.

Be particularly alert for opportunities to promote socializing if you have volunteer assignments that don't involve any human interaction. Mary Vaughan manages volunteers who work in single-person shifts. "The only time they would maybe interact with each other is when they change shifts, but two people could be MobileMed volunteers for years and never relieve each other." She knew this might not only lead to boredom, but also could make the volunteers feel isolated, so she looked for opportunities for volunteers to spend time together to give them a chance to socialize and meet people that they didn't know.[12] Socializing also provides a way for volunteers to share ideas, solve mutual problems, and create better ways of organizing workflow or communicating.

If you have meetings on a recurring basis, consider allotting a half hour before the meeting's scheduled start for an optional social period. Those who are all business can use that time for short committee meetings or skip them all together. Those who enjoy socializing can get together with other volunteers. You might also set aside one meeting a year for a family picnic, party, or dinner, or offer a social event in addition to the regular meetings.

You may also want to set aside some time to socialize with the volunteers. Taking a volunteer to coffee or lunch is an excellent way not only to show appreciation, but also to create a casual environment in which the volunteer will feel more comfortable sharing any questions or concerns. If you have too many volunteers for one-on-one meetings to be feasible, consider spending time with a project team or working group—something as simple as having pizza after a meeting can give people a real sense of being appreciated.

Tia Milne found a way to recognize and reward volunteers while improving staff-volunteer relations and providing an environment for socializing. "From Thanksgiving through Christmas," she explains, "we asked the staff to bring in snacks and things for the volunteers and during the break to go in and talk to them. And we didn't ask just the volunteer team but we asked the entire staff—all different departments ... it took maybe 20 or 30 minutes of staff time ... and we heard from a lot of volunteers that that actually meant more to them than any [larger] sort of appreciation ... because they got to hear from other food bank people, they got to learn more about the food bank, and they just enjoyed that interaction."[13]

Although a friendly atmosphere is enjoyable, not every volunteer will want to devote significant amounts of time to socializing. Some volunteers have limited time available, want to be as productive as possible, and don't want to waste time on inconsequential activities. Try to balance these two points of view by providing opportunities to socialize that do not detract from task work.

EXPRESSING THANKS AND GIVING PRAISE

Recognize achievement but praise the person.

—James C. Fisher and Kathleen M. Cole[14]

Praise doesn't cost anything, it's easy, and it's one of the best things you can do to motivate and retain volunteers. Never pass up an opportunity to say "thanks," "good job," or "well done." If possible, say it multiple times, in different ways. Say it in person, send an email, and follow it up with a handwritten note. Plaques and awards banquets are fine, but don't overlook the power of ongoing recognition and repeated reminders that you value the volunteer's time and contributions.

It is almost impossible to thank people too much. Thanking tells people that their efforts were noted and appreciated. The feeling of being appreciated is one of the major reasons people volunteer, and in a sense, thanking is the currency by which you pay volunteers for their work.

There are good ways to thank people and not-so-good ways. The not-so-good ways are the dismissive "thanks" that is reminiscent of the boss thanking the secretary for a cup of coffee, the printed thanks in the annual report (without any in-person show of appreciation), and the "thanks, but ... " kind of thanks that wraps the "thank you" in the paper that held yesterday's fish, as in "Thanks, but next time could you do it faster?"

Be observant of what individual volunteers enjoy doing, find pleasurable, fear, and avoid. Some people are rewarded by something that is torture for others (e.g., receiving an award in front of a crowd). Gary Chapman and Paul White identified "the 5 languages of appreciation in the workplace" as words of affirmation, tangible gifts, quality time, acts of service, and physical touch.[15] Acts of service could be something like coworkers or paid staff pitching in to help, while quality time might be time spent one-on-one with the supervisor contributing ideas.

The best way to thank volunteers is to do it as quickly as possible following their actions and make it as specific as possible to their actions ("Thank you for taking the evening shift on such short notice—we were able to stay open and assist 10 clients" rather than just "Thanks for working last night"). Thank volunteers whenever they do something they should be thanked for, even if it seems repetitive. Whenever possible, show volunteers the value of their work ("Wow, your phone calls brought in nearly $500 in ticket sales"). You can also be specific in your praise by complimenting personal traits as well as actions ("You always work so well with our older patients" or "You are so good at math").

A simple procedure you can initiate that ensures each volunteer gets thanked at least once a year is to send birthday cards. If you include birthdate (day and month) on the volunteer application form, it's easy enough to create a spreadsheet or tickler file by date to remind yourself which cards go out when. In addition to birthday wishes, include a thank you for their volunteer service. Some managers use holiday cards for this purpose, but I think birthday cards are better not only because people celebrate different holidays, but also because the recipient feels singled out and not part of a bulk mailing. If you do send cards out in a group, try to write a short personal message on each one.

The most meaningful thank-you messages are specific and personal:

Not so good: Thank you for your service, team.

Better: Thank you Tom, for all the great work you do.

Best: Thank you, Tom, for the great job you do greeting museum patrons. You make visitors feel welcome from the moment they step inside.

A particularly effective way to thank volunteers is to praise them to other people, whether or not the volunteer is actually present. You may remember as a child hearing your mom or dad brag about you to another parent. Remember that sense of pride? Well, you can give that feeling to a deserving volunteer. Even if the volunteer doesn't hear the compliment, you can bet word will get back.

Another way of recognizing value is simply to connect with the volunteer as a person. Tia Milne routinely works with 100 volunteers or more at a time. In that environment, it is easy for a volunteer—even a committed volunteer who comes in on a scheduled basis—to feel like just another warm body. Milne advises other managers to "listen to the volunteers and make sure they know that they are an important piece and that you're not just kind of shuffling them through. Like remembering the simplest things about them or their life or their family means so much more than a special sticker that you can put on their sign-in sheet or something."[16]

REWARDS

If you're going to reward volunteers, make sure what you are doing is actually a reward. It seems as though this would go without saying, but unfortunately, I have seen too many examples of rewards that were not, in fact, rewards. Here are some examples:

- A reward that costs the volunteer money. A well-known cancer center sent out invitations to a volunteer recognition brunch. How nice, thought the volunteer opening the invitation. Wait! What's this? The RSVP card says that the charge for the brunch is $10. So let me understand this. I'm paying you. To reward me. (Instead of rewarding the volunteer, this organization managed to insult him instead.)

  Holding a volunteer recognition event that forces the person to miss work, drive a long distance (gas money), buy or rent clothing (such as a tuxedo or a costume), or hire a babysitter also costs the volunteer money. Giving a gift certificate or pass that requires a larger purchase or entry fee likewise is not a good way to reward.

- A reward that is too small to be meaningful. Unless the volunteers are teenagers, a gift certificate for a McDonald's Happy Meal is not a reward. If you don't have the money for something the volunteer will appreciate, make up a nice certificate and provide plenty of heartfelt gratitude instead.

- A reward that is not welcome. A 12-inch-tall hourglass with a brass name plate shows appreciation but may not be that welcome a gift (what do I do with *this*?). Gifts that are obviously expensive but frivolous may make volunteers wonder whether the money would have been better spent furthering the goals of the organization.

• A reward that is embarrassing. This category covers a lot of ground: gifts that are overly personal, gag gifts that aren't funny to the recipient, rewards that place the volunteer in an awkward position or that give a shy person public exposure, rewards that are out of scale to the accomplishment, gifts that are insensitive (bottle of wine to someone who doesn't drink), and rewards that are late in coming. Oh, and take this from someone with the name Sakaduski, check and double check the spelling of a volunteer's name before engraving it in brass.

THE ELEMENT OF FUN

Part of the responsibility of a volunteer manager is to create a good experience for the volunteer. While this may seem somewhat unimportant, it can be critical to volunteer retention.

The attitude of the manager is a good place to start. "It's key," says Mary Vaughan. "It's key to everything. It's key to any leadership, in my mind. Key to any leadership position or management position . . . if people think you're excited, they feel like they're coming on board something that is worthwhile, gratifying, they get to meet other people, and they get to do good work . . . I actually would say enthusiasm and communication are probably key, and respect for their work—appreciation for their work."[17]

Look for opportunities to make the volunteer experience more fun. Having a summer clean-up day? Provide a garden sprinkler for volunteers to run through to cool off! Finishing a mailing? Order pizza! Jazz up group activities like painting or gardening with an energizing music soundtrack. Open a meeting with a short game, funny poem, or trivia question. Come up with a fun theme for your volunteer appreciation event. For example, have an Academy Awards–style event with a red carpet and arrange for a few volunteers to play paparazzi. Just remember that not everyone likes to be the star, so don't force people to dress up or participate in skits.

Consider competition—but only if it's a natural fit and can be done constructively. Dan Gabor says: "With some volunteers, competition is something that can really backfire in your face. Some people are naturally competitive . . . others just immediately retreat into an 'I'm not going to win anything, so why bother?' "[18]

Think about something more fun than standard certificates and plaques. An animal care organization might give an award shaped like a dog bone; a neighborhood beautification team might win "the golden trowel." You can glue small objects to plaques, use gold spray paint, or repurpose children's toys to create novel one-of-a-kind awards for volunteers. Dollar stores can be a great source of inspiration.

If your annual meeting tends to be dull, consider bringing in an interesting speaker or creating a slide show set to music. I like to hold a year-end meeting that features a slide show of pictures from all the volunteer activities and projects during that year. People enjoy seeing themselves and their teammates in action, and it reminds everyone of how much they've accomplished.

Ever see kids scramble for free candy thrown during a parade? Is the candy that big a treat for them? No. Parade candy is exciting because it's free and it's fun. You can do the same thing by adding some simple games (with prizes), giveaways, door prizes, free tickets, or raffles to your annual meeting or appreciation event.

SENSE OF ACCOMPLISHMENT

One of the best and most satisfying rewards volunteers can get is to see that their efforts resulted in a substantive result. In some cases, the result of the volunteer's effort is self-evident or perhaps there is no tangible benefit, but if there is a result that can be shown to the volunteer, be sure to take advantage of it.

Volunteers who work to develop a project or activity should be invited to observe the implementation of that effort. For example, if the volunteers worked to establish a school-based program, see if they might be allowed to observe the children participating. At the very least, give them photographs, children's artwork, or thank-you notes from the students or teachers. If volunteers worked on a fund drive to raise money for a building addition, make sure they are invited to the groundbreaking and dedication. People who labored on a book sale should be sent a photograph of the stack of books and materials the library was able to purchase with the funds they raised.

With their permission, mention volunteers by name and show photographs of them at work when you post information about new programs or facilities on the organization's Facebook page or in other outlets. Use press releases to publicize the accomplishments of the volunteer program and include names of the volunteers (with their permission) who helped. Use quantitative measures whenever possible ("brought in 143 new members," "raised $5,000," "distributed 680 pounds of food").

Volunteers feel inspired when they know their efforts are paying off. Jim Starr says, "I think one of the things that attracts a lot of people to volunteer with the ARC [American Red Cross] is the fact that as a volunteer they get to have a direct impact on the lives of others who have been impacted by disasters. They get to provide their service direct, face to face, eyeball to eyeball with those that have been impacted and there's a great deal of satisfaction that our volunteers get from that experience."[19]

Volunteers are donors of time, and they deserve to be recognized for their contributions, just as donors of money are. Tia Milne advises: "Always remember that these are people who are giving up their time and they do want to make a difference. I think it's easy to sometimes to just lose sight of that because we're caught up in so many things."[20]

QUESTIONS TO GET YOU STARTED

1. What are the main reasons volunteers leave your organization, and are there ways you could do a better job of retaining volunteers?
2. What could you do to create a better sense of empowerment for the volunteers?
3. What could you do to inspire a greater feeling of belonging and more opportunity for personal growth within the organization?
4. Can you think of any other ways you could reward volunteers?
5. Are there ways you could improve the volunteer experience?
6. How could you help volunteers better realize the part they play in the overall mission of your organization?

CHAPTER 9

Potential Problems and How to Avoid Them

Most people spend more time and energy going around problems than in trying to solve them.

—Henry Ford[1]

HANDLING PROBLEMS AND COMPLAINTS

As any public relations professional (and a long list of politicians) will tell you, it is never a good idea to try to hide a problem—or worse—lie about it. No matter how big the issue, you are almost always better off getting it out in the open and dealing with it. Neither unaddressed problems nor spoiled fish improve with time. The size of the problem and the number of people affected will determine the steps you must take, but here is a logical approach for dealing with a significant problem. The faster these steps are completed, the better.

1. Determine the nature and extent of the problem. (Investigate thoroughly and get input from everyone who was involved.)
2. As quickly as possible, limit the spread of the damage—if necessary, even before you have completed step one.
3. Identify the immediate and potential impacts and the affected parties.
4. Define an action plan for addressing the problem, preventing further damage, and remediating the damage done.

5. Make a statement (in a forum that will reach all concerned parties) to outline the problem, its impact, and your plan for addressing it. Depending on the nature of the problem, you may want an attorney to review the statement in advance and advise you accordingly.

6. Listen (allow people to complain, express anger, make suggestions, and ask questions) in a concerned but unemotional manner and in an environment that allows free expression.

7. Respond to questions and comments without being angry, defensive, or judgmental.

8. If you don't know the answer, say you don't know the answer.

9. If you know the answer but are prohibited from answering, say that you cannot answer.

10. Demonstrate a commitment to addressing the problem, putting policies in place to prevent similar problems in the future, and allowing people to continue to contact you with questions or concerns.

11. Be alert for rumors, misinformation, and political infighting in the wake of a problem and be prepared to address them immediately.

12. If a volunteer made a mistake that led to the problem, counsel the volunteer about what could have been done differently and how to handle similar situations in the future. Document this conversation in the volunteer's file.

When you are counseling a volunteer who has made a significant mistake, hold the discussion in a nonthreatening place. Rather than a "come into my office" kind of talk, you may have better results with a "let's meet for coffee" at a convenient (to the volunteer) location. This generally inspires a more honest and casual discussion, which may produce better results. Nobody likes to feel that they are in trouble. By fostering a "let's solve this together" attitude, you will minimize defensiveness and encourage cooperation.

Sometimes, the problem is not a specific mistake or accident but a general complaint—about a program, policy, staff member, another volunteer, or even yourself. When receiving a complaint, express concern and ask for more information, without either accepting the report at face value or becoming defensive. Then gather additional facts from other sources. Once you have a more complete understanding of the situation, you can begin to determine whether there is a problem, and if there is, start to formulate a plan for how to handle it.

Sometimes, a complaint springs from a simple misunderstanding. If this is the case, do not make the volunteer feel stupid. Even if it was not your fault, it may be face-saving for you to gently take the blame, for example, "Sorry I wasn't clear about that. The new hours are 1 to 5 p.m., not 1 to 5 a.m." A misunderstanding on the part of one volunteer may indicate that other volunteers are confused. In that case, you may want to respond with, "I'm sure glad you brought this up. I will send an email to the group to set the record straight."

Most people find email the easiest way to voice a problem, and because they don't have to face you in person, they will be less inhibited. So your initial indication that there is a problem could come in the form of an innocent looking email that contains an angry message from a disgruntled volunteer who has, unbeknownst to you, been stewing for some time. In other words, place your tray table in the upright position and fasten your seatbelt. You're in for a bumpy ride.

Read the message carefully, and then read it again. Make sure you have heard and understood what the person is saying. Do not immediately let loose an angry response. Take a deep breath (even walk away for a minute or two if you have to) before beginning to draft a response. Sometimes, the best approach is to simply pick up the phone and call, but do this when you have a cool head and allow a little time to pass so that the volunteer has cooled down as well.

Acknowledge the person's point of view and feelings. Do not attempt to discredit or argue at this point. Phrases such as "you shouldn't be angry about that," or "that's not what happened at all," will not get you the outcome you want. Instead, try "I hear your frustration" or "I can understand why you would feel that way." This does not indicate that the person is correct, only that you respect the volunteer's point of view. Your goal at this point is not to get the person to back down or agree that you are right. Your goal is to calm the person down, assure the person that you are listening, and begin to build a bridge toward a solution.

If several people are involved, the situation is a little trickier. Try to hear all parties' concerns and acknowledge the validity of their opinions: "I can see where Sarah is coming from, but I understand Jim's frustration as well." Notice that you are not saying either one is in the right.

If you have repeated problems with the same volunteers, it probably indicates a personality issue that will need to be addressed. Counsel the battling volunteers separately. Encourage them to work it out privately. Providing a coliseum environment will only ensure that the lions are well fed. If necessary, reassign the volunteers so that they need not work together.

PREJUDICE/BIAS/HARASSMENT

As a manager, you have a moral and legal obligation to provide a workplace that is free from hostility and harassment. This means that everyone in the organization treats other volunteers, staff members, and constituents in a respectful way, regardless of their race, age, nationality, religion, gender, sexual orientation, or social status.

As mentioned previously, you should cover this topic during orientation and include it in your policy statement. Make your expectations clear. After that, be observant for any behaviors that are in violation of your policy and address them immediately. If you wait, the person may forget (or deny) what was said or done. Constructive criticism should be provided privately, in a tactful but clear way, and should focus on the behavior, not the person.

Wrong: "I see you are prejudiced against Muslims . . . "

Better: "That joke you just told is not acceptable in our organization. We do not allow volunteers to make jokes about people's religious beliefs or nationalities."

The volunteer may be embarrassed and try to make light of the situation, perhaps suggesting that you are being silly or oversensitive. Explain that what starts as a joke can lead to a hostile work environment, and that is unacceptable. These kinds of problems can not only result in volunteers leaving, but can also open the organization up to lawsuits. Depending on the severity of the situation, give the volunteer an opportunity to apologize and acknowledge that he or she understands the behavior was inappropriate, but make it clear that the volunteer will be dismissed if the behavior is repeated. Document the conversation and observe the volunteer carefully.

In addition to inappropriate jokes, unacceptable behaviors include mocking religious customs or dress, treating people differently because of their socioeconomic level, stereotyping people based on their race or other characteristics, making comments about people's sexual orientation or gender, using derogatory language or slurs, making threats or unwelcome sexual advances, and making fun of a disability or mental condition. These actions can be made through written notes, emails, texts, posts, tweets, unwelcome gifts, gestures or physical contact, verbal remarks, or phone calls.

This is another situation in which having a written policy that all volunteers read and sign when they join the organization can help prevent problems. And even if a problem occurs, you have solid ground from which to point out the infraction.

VOLUNTEERS VERSUS PAID STAFF

Problems between paid staff and volunteers often arise from failing to develop the volunteer program with input from staff and not obtaining their support early in the process. If staff members see volunteers as an imposition, or have had volunteer workers foisted on them, there is little chance for a good outcome. Their reactions can range from subtle tactics like being late for meetings to outright sabotage.

When the volunteer program is an integral part of the organization's activities and when volunteers and paid staff work as partners toward a common goal, problems are few. However, if volunteers are disrespectful to staff members and staff members treat volunteers as unimportant unskilled laborers, there will be problems.

Even seemingly subtle practices can send a message that the organization does not value its volunteers. Susan Ellis, who has spent 35 years advising volunteer-involving organizations, has identified some examples of ways volunteers are sometimes treated like second-class citizens by staff members, which can create bad feelings:

- Putting essential information on an intranet or password-protected website where volunteers cannot access it
- Making volunteers search for a work space instead of setting aside a dedicated area, proper equipment, and materials
- Not providing an official email address (or letterhead stationery) to a volunteer who is doing research or outreach as a representative of the organization
- Not providing a secure area in which volunteers can leave personal items while on duty
- Not inviting volunteers engaged in a project to meetings about that project[2]

Another source of friction can be the volunteers' perception that they are working hard to raise money, and that the staff members are then taking that money (as salaries) rather than letting it go toward the organization's activities. The paid staff may also feel threatened and worried that volunteers will take their jobs. These problems can be prevented by determining in advance the tasks best done by paid staff and then clearly delineating these from tasks to be performed by volunteers. The roles and responsibilities should be mutually defined and agreed upon, and then reinforced during orientation and training.

Problems between volunteers and staff members are best dealt with immediately, before personality disputes become vendettas. While you can't force people to like each other, or even to work together, you can try to encourage cooperation.

The first step is to identify the problem. Is it a single staff person or everyone in the office? Does it boil down to control issues? Worries about the quality of work? Fear of losing their jobs? Not wanting to take the time to deal with volunteers?

Many of these problems can be headed off by providing orientation for staff members as well as for volunteers. Let the paid staff know what tasks the volunteers will be performing and why. Request that staff members not assign volunteers additional tasks without consulting with you first. Explain how important encouragement and gratitude are as the currencies for compensating volunteers. Make it clear that while staff members may, in certain situations, be in a position to supervise volunteers, you will make sure the volunteers are trained and are performing their tasks well, and you will address any problem situations so that working with volunteers will not make additional work for the staff.

If staff members will be supervising volunteers directly, provide them with some training. Keep in mind that people who have never supervised others may not be familiar with how to motivate workers, how to give constructive criticism, or even how to reinforce good behaviors. Most professionals, even those who frequently come into contact with volunteers such as teachers, nurses, and social workers, were not taught these skills as part of their training.

On the flip side, tell volunteers who the staff members are and what they do. Make sure the volunteers are respectful of the paid staff, and reinforce your desire that volunteers and staff work cooperatively for the benefit of the organization and its goals. Explain to volunteers that criticisms are welcome but should be addressed to you, not to staff members. Staff members do not work for volunteers. Like volunteers, they work for the organization.

Do not tolerate "us versus them" attitudes. Educate staff members and volunteers about the contributions each make and the fact that, together, they make the organization succeed. This is not *competition*, it is *cooperation*. To encourage cooperation, there must be information sharing, honesty, communication, and mutual respect. Phrases such as "they always" and "we never" should be banished to make room for "how can we all . . ."

It will help if you do a little internal marketing of the volunteer program. Make sure the staff is aware of the volunteers' contributions. Post newspaper articles about their work, include staff members in volunteer appreciation events, make staff members aware when volunteers hit service milestones, and create an annual report that describes the volunteers' activities, the number of hours that were given, and the value of that donated time.

COMMON TYPES OF PROBLEM VOLUNTEERS

Here are some common problem volunteers that managers have to deal with:

- *The Pea Shooter.* This is the person who, just when you are feeling most confident, takes a clean shot from the sidelines. To see a great example, watch the movie *Christmas Vacation.* After Clark Griswold has spent hours and hours setting up his dream-come-true lighting display and has the family gathered on the front lawn for the grand unveiling ("drumroll please"), his father-in-law points out "the lights aren't twinkling, Clark." I had a similar experience when I enthusiastically presented a new brochure series in a large meeting, only to have the pea shooter of the group stand up and point out a typographical error in one of the brochures. Pea shooters were never told by their mothers, "If you don't have anything nice to say, don't say anything at all." They seem to relish pointing out the flaws of others, usually in the most public settings, and in the most embarrassing circumstances. This can range from minor back-seat driving to an all-out assault on the way you do things.Although it is difficult not to take offense, become angry, be defensive, or, say, strangle the person in the parking lot after the meeting, the pea shooter is best neutralized gently, immediately, and publicly. "Thanks so much for pointing that out, Clarice," you might cheerfully say and then quickly move on to another topic. Try to separate out constructive criticism or suggestions that have been clumsily offered but well intended from intentional undermining.

- *Negative Ned.* Ned never met a silver lining he couldn't turn inside-out into a dark cloud. In the eyes of these naysayers, nothing is ever right. While negativity is more of an annoyance than anything, if it is left to fester it can affect morale and even (if the volunteer is in contact with the public) harm the organization's image and reputation. Counsel the volunteer to address this attitude and put a plan in place for correcting the behavior. Make expectations clear and explain the consequences of failing to meet them.

- *The Bulletproof Volunteer.* These volunteers may have a special position, connection, or status (donated money, family connections, professional credentials, specialized skill), or may simply have been with the organization a long time or provided such valuable service that they feel the organization cannot survive without them. It's a difficult problem to address because these folks have (or think they have) status that not only outranks other volunteers but also outranks you. You can approach the director or board and attempt to get some support, but if the volunteer really is essential to the organization, you will probably be told to "work it out." Your only other option is to go to the volunteer and be honest about your concerns: "I realize you are invaluable to our organization, but the other volunteers are having a difficult time with your getting privileges they don't have. How do you think we can work through this?" By emphasizing your mutual goal (the success of the organization) you may at least get the volunteer to be less strident and more accommodating to the needs of others.

- *The Know-It-All.* Know-it-alls have an answer for everything and are quick to offer suggestions, criticisms, and words of wisdom to others. Sometimes the know-it-all's advice is helpful, but it may be clumsily offered or offered too freely. This can create issues with staff members as well as other volunteers. Know-it-alls make others less likely to offer their opinions, stifle open discussions, and alienate others.In public situations, address the know-it-all respectfully but firmly. "Thank you, Al. That's an interesting suggestion. Does anyone else have any ideas?" You may have to interrupt, but even this can be done tactfully. "Al, I'm sorry to stop you, but we only have an hour and I'd like to get everyone's input. Perhaps we can chat after the meeting." When you talk with know-it-alls privately, explain that they are coming on a little strong and, while their contributions are valued, they need to respect other people's ideas as well. You may want to point out that other people will be more receptive to their input if they offer it more selectively and in a more respectful way.

- *The Power Monger.* Power mongers push other volunteers (and even staff members) around, dismiss those whom they view as inconsequential, and grab every bit of turf they can. These volunteers often have large egos that need continual stroking and a seemingly unquenchable thirst for control.Volunteers who are motivated by power make excellent committee heads and project managers if they can be reined in (sometimes a big "if"). Start by being very clear about boundaries of responsibility and what you are willing to authorize them to do. Keep a sharp eye on them, communicating frequently to make sure their trajectory matches what you had in mind. Provide honest, clear feedback, while not backing down from your position of authority. Above all, do not let this type of volunteer push you around, or you are in for a long merry-go-round ride.

- *The Loose Cannon.* This volunteer repeatedly makes decisions, takes actions, and directs others without proper authorization. Loose cannons ignore policies and procedures, defy orders, create their own rules, and have an attitude that they know what's best and therefore can ignore guidelines they don't agree with.If you allow the loose cannon to get away with this type of behavior, you are setting a poor example for other volunteers and potentially putting the organization at risk. This is another time when it pays to have a clearly worded position description, preferably one that the volunteer has signed to indicate his or her agreement.The real danger here is that the volunteer strays into territory that opens the organization up to liability issues. A volunteer that exceeds authority by signing a liability release, ordering materials (or buying them with the expectation of reimbursement), or obligating the organization in some other way can get you into real trouble. If you have a volunteer who does not respect the limits you impose, you will need to dismiss the volunteer.

- *The Undependable Volunteer.* This person shows up late, shows up intermittently, or doesn't show up at all. Sometimes, the undependable volunteer is simply overcommitted, disorganized, or under stress. Other times, the volunteer is actually inept. By being inefficient, disorganized, or distracted, the undependable volunteer misses deadlines and doesn't do the things you thought were being done.Mary Vaughan had a volunteer fail to show up for her shift for registering patients for the MobileMed van. The situation was particularly bad because the shifts had only one volunteer assigned, so when someone doesn't show up, it means there is no one to help the medical professionals who have set up the mobile clinic to treat patients. She says that it can happen occasionally, by accident, with even the most responsible volunteers, but if it's happening because the volunteer has a different value system and is not reliable, she lets the volunteer go. She explained to the person, "People have jobs, people have appointments to go to, people do have things that they're obligated to . . . so I really expect that you take it seriously and be there, because we count on you to be there."[3]

- *The Over-Promiser*. These are the volunteers you were most excited about. Over-promisers talk a great game, volunteer for many activities, are filled with enthusiasm, and are eager to take on huge projects single-handedly. Unfortunately, their promises never seem to pan out. Time passes, deadlines are missed, and you have to keep following up to find out what is going on. Sometimes, the over-promiser meant well and actually believed that he or she could accomplish what was promised, but then something happened that prevented this from happening. In this situation, the volunteer is likely embarrassed and feels worse than you do. The situation can sometimes be salvaged by speaking with the volunteer and together working out a more reasonable set of tasks and expectations. Other times, over-promisers cannot accurately estimate effort or allocate time, or compulsively start numerous projects but lose interest quickly. In these cases, you must limit activities assigned to the volunteer and monitor progress carefully. If the volunteer continues to have problems or close supervision is not possible, you will have to tell the volunteer to find a more suitable placement.

- *The Burned Out Volunteer*. Some people have too much going on in their lives or have personal pressures that weigh heavily on them. Others take on too many volunteer assignments, work too many hours, or have simply been working in the same capacity for too long. The result is burnout. Here are some of the signs:
  - Volunteer seems tired and frustrated
  - Volunteer fails to fulfill responsibilities
  - Volunteer misses meetings
  - Volunteer is increasingly unable to make a positive contribution to the organization
  - Volunteer complains of physical stress (headaches, insomnia, etc.)

Most volunteers will not ask to have their duties reduced. Instead, they will struggle for a period of time and then withdraw completely. Be alert for signs of burnout and work with the volunteer to reduce the stresses before you lose the volunteer.

WHEN A VOLUNTEER DOESN'T WORK OUT

Sometimes, it is clear that a volunteer placement is not working. Other times, you are not aware there is a problem until the volunteer resigns. If the volunteer has asked to leave, find out as much as you can about his or her reasons. By the time volunteers announce their intentions, they usually have their minds made up, but occasionally you can resolve the problem that led to their decision.

If the volunteer is leaving for personal reasons (health, family issues, work demands), express empathy and indicate your interest in having the volunteer return if the situation changes. You may even want to ask if you can place the volunteer on "inactive" status, which makes the decision seem less final. Inactive volunteers should receive communications such as newsletters that keep them up to date with the organization but should be taken off broadcast lists so that they are not bothered with routine issues that no longer concern them.

If the volunteer has not asked to leave but is not performing well, you should deal with it in a progressive way, starting with a counseling session that includes clear instructions for improvement (which you should document in the file), followed by a written warning, then temporary or permanent suspension, depending on the severity of the case. In most cases, the situation will likely not move beyond the written warning stage because the volunteer will either improve or will leave on his or her own. People generally do not want to stay in an unpaid position when they know they are not doing a good job.

Complications arise when volunteers are given mixed messages, either by you or by different people. If more than one person is giving the volunteer direction, the supervisors must first agree on the nature of the problem and what should be done. Ultimately, it is your responsibility to both the organization and the volunteer to be clear about whether the volunteer is performing properly, and if not, what the options are. It is not fair to either party to prolong a bad situation or to give false hope to a volunteer who has been poorly matched to the assignment.

Criticism is almost never welcomed, but it can be done in a positive way. First, criticize the behavior, not the person. Second, make your expectations and the repercussions of failing to meet them clear. Be supportive and encouraging, but firm. Do not be drawn into debates. Use specific examples of behavior you yourself have observed or point to measurable criteria that have not been met. This is where having a position description with goals can be helpful. Make specific suggestions about how the volunteer can improve and provide a reasonable time frame in which the improvements should be accomplished.

Possible solutions for problem volunteers include:

- *Reassignment.* The volunteer may not be a good fit for the assignment, or there may be a personality issue with another volunteer or a staff member. Moving the volunteer to a different location or changing the responsibilities may be all that is needed to correct the situation. It may also be that the volunteer is not able to handle the tasks, pressures, or responsibilities of the position. Talking with the volunteer to share your concerns and listening to the volunteer's perceptions of the situation may help uncover the problem and lead you toward a solution.

• *Temporary suspension or leave.* Relieving a volunteer temporarily may be the solution for a health or family issue, outside work conflict, or addiction issue (assuming the volunteer is seeking treatment). If the issue is not temporary, a temporary fix is not the answer, as the problem will recur when the volunteer returns. Make expectations clear when offering a temporary suspension or leave.

• *Referral to another organization or location.* If the problem relates to something unique to your organization or location and the volunteer is otherwise a good worker, you may want to make a referral to another organization or move the volunteer to a different facility. For example, a volunteer at an animal shelter who has developed a dog allergy may not be able to work at your facility but might make an excellent library assistant. Do not, however, pass on problem volunteers. This does no one a service, as it only makes problems for another organization and creates additional frustration for the volunteer.

• *Dismissal.* Letting a volunteer go should be a last choice and undertaken only when you have made several attempts to address the problem, unless the volunteer has violated a stated policy or made a serious error of judgment that you feel warrants immediate dismissal.

Dismissing a volunteer can be a very difficult experience for a manager. The process can be made easier by having a clearly established progression, starting with a discussion as soon as a problem is identified, and escalating through conversations about why performance isn't improving. Ideally, if no solution (change of responsibilities or scheduling, additional training, different work environment) proves successful, it will become apparent to both the volunteer and the manager that the placement is not working out.

If the volunteer must be dismissed unwillingly, explain why the action is being taken and be clear that the individual is no longer in the volunteer program. Retrieve any keys, name badges, or passes and remove the volunteer from the contact lists used by you and others in the organization. If the volunteer complains to other volunteers, you may need to acknowledge that the volunteer was let go but resist making any personal remarks or sharing any details.

These situations should be dealt with in a private setting and documented. You should be as specific as possible in describing the problem behavior and be clear that you are letting the volunteer go. Allow the volunteer to object or express anger, but do not be persuaded to change your decision merely because of the volunteer's reaction to dismissal. Any waffling will only postpone the inevitable and create additional hard feelings.

PREPARING FOR YOUR DEPARTURE

Leaders don't create followers, they create more leaders.

—Tom Peters[4]

If you manage volunteers, part of your job is to prepare the organization for the day you leave. You may feel heroic as a one-man band, but you are not doing the organization any favors. Any group, no matter how small, is at risk if it relies too heavily on a single individual. The organization not only must be prepared for the day the person who manages the volunteers retires or takes another job, but also should have a plan in place for the unexpected loss of that person.

One way to do this is to identify volunteers with leadership skills and put them in positions such as committee chair or project team leader that allow them to gain experience and learn the operation of the volunteer program. You should also think about moving these people around so that they know more than just one part of the organization. Even if there is no one who would be willing or able to step in as manager, a shared knowledge base can be invaluable to a new hire who may have volunteer management skills but does not know how your particular organization operates.

A succession plan (a plan for what happens after you leave) provides continuity for the organization. Part of this plan is infrastructure: forms, policies, procedures, and best practices. If this structure is already in place, the organization can continue to operate effectively, even under initially inexperienced leadership.

Maureen Eccleston believes this is the fundamental requirement for a successful volunteer organization anyway. "I really think it all comes back to having a high quality, structured volunteer program so that when the volunteers come in, they know what they're going to be doing, they know why they are doing it, they know how they're going to contribute to the bigger problem, and all of those pieces enable them to want to keep coming back to contribute more, to maybe bring friends or colleagues to volunteer with them, and hopefully even become donors. So I think it really comes down to having a structured program in place."[5]

GETTING HELP

If you are new to volunteer management, it's easy to feel a little overwhelmed. You may have come from a job where you never had to run a meeting, manage people, create schedules, or oversee projects. Or maybe this is your first job. Even experienced managers sometimes have questions, face new situations, or have problems for which they need assistance. Fortunately, there are many places where you can get help. Let's start with some guidance from the experts:

"Look for advice from within the [volunteer] sector," suggests Tony Goodrow, "but equally look for advice outside." He recommends books on communication, organization, and motivation. "I understand that employees and volunteers are completely different in nature but there are some core pieces of practice and theory and strategy that can help, regardless of the situation . . . If you think of books like *Getting Things Done* or *7 Habits of Highly Successful People*, they weren't written for the volunteer sector, but they've got great advice that can be applied in a volunteer position."[6] Mary Vaughan agrees. "People are people, and if you're going to coordinate volunteers, it's a management position. You're going to have similar problems to any management position."[7]

Networking provides many ways to get support, get questions answered, and find new and better ways of doing things. Sites such as LinkedIn have groups that allow you to meet and share experiences with other people who manage volunteers. Meghan Kaskoun suggests, "Get connected with your local association of volunteer managers so that you have a support network in your city." She also recommends the Cybervpm online discussion group for volunteer managers. "It's getting connected with the resources that are out there and educating yourself on what good volunteer management looks like."[8]

There are many websites that offer volunteer management tools, references, best practices, recruitment aids, and a variety of other resources, most of which are free. Links for these sites are listed in Chapter 10.

WHAT THE FUTURE HOLDS

So with vast changes in technology, an evolving volunteer workforce, reductions in program funding, and increasing community need, where are volunteer programs heading and how can the volunteer manager prepare? "The pace of change in our life today is so vast," says Goodrow. "The key skill is going to be adaptability. What we often think of Darwin as saying is survival of the fittest, but what he was really talking about was survival of those who are most adaptable."[9]

For one thing, the volunteers themselves are changing—in who they are, how they approach volunteering, and what they want to do. Tia Milne says: "I think there are more volunteers looking to use their professional skills in the volunteer world ... And I think that as nonprofits we're kind of struggling with that a little bit because that's not what we're used to, so we haven't really developed those positions as well as they could be."[10]

Tony Goodrow talks about tapping the educated pool of people who are retired. "They want to make a difference and they have a skill set, the expertise, to execute more change at the strategic level than at the task level ... a change that I've heard talked about in the sector is the flip from staff doing the strategic work and volunteers stuffing the envelopes to volunteers doing the strategic work and hiring people to stuff the envelopes."[11]

Volunteerism in general seems to be on an uptick and there are more ways for volunteers to contribute and to do so on their own terms. Ronna Charles Branch says: "Volunteerism seems to be increasing ... I think people in general just want to do better for their communities."[12] "There's a lot more one time or episodic volunteers," says Maureen Eccleston. "They had Mrs. Smith, who comes every Wednesday from three till five, and that's her volunteer schedule. Well, the new Mrs. Smith doesn't want to come every Wednesday from three till five. She wants to have a specific task that she has to do and maybe she does it at home or maybe she does it in the office, and once she's done she's going to go to another organization. So, short term, more episodic, less ongoing consistent volunteer opportunities is really the big, big trend right now, which is challenging for a lot of organizations."[13]

Meghan Kaskoun has also seen the impact busy schedules are having. "The trend has gone from long-term volunteering where we could get volunteers to stay in a position for the course of a few years and now younger volunteers are coming in and wanting to volunteer in different ways. They may volunteer by tweeting for an organization or trying to fundraise for an organization completely off-site, in electronic ways."[14]

Maureen Eccleston thinks organizations will increasingly have to deal with short-term volunteers. "People are not as interested in staying at an organization for 30 years just like you don't see people doing that in the workforce so much anymore ... instead, people are hopping around a bit more." She sees this as part of a larger trend. "Where the evolving takes place is in the same way that we're seeing in the nonprofit sector and even the private sector, which is people doing a bazillion different things—having many, many, multiple hats as we continue to try and meet bigger needs with smaller budgets."[15]

Tony Goodrow says, "I think the one [trend] that sticks out the most, that I think is going to be the most relevant, is the ability to self-organize. If I want a volunteer to do something, I'm not going to need a standard structure in which it has to happen. Put a group of like-minded people together, they'll try to execute something and they will, quite possibly, disband after the project is fulfilled." "They just want to go get something done," Goodrow explains. "They don't want to jump through a lot of hoops to make it happen. 'I just want to go clean up the park. What do you mean I have to get a police check done? Never mind, I'm not going to volunteer for the city. I'm going to put a group up on Facebook and get all my buddies out and we're just going to go out on Saturday and clean the park.'"[16]

There may also be changes in the profession. Meghan Kaskoun says, "Since I've been in volunteer management there has always been an underlying current of frustration with not being seen as a recognized profession, and we have been trying to work on that for years."[17] She adds: "Volunteer management has struggled to have that same level of recognition not just from other professional associations/societies but often within our own organizations. I believe that is why our ability in the United States of America to create support networks (i.e. Cybervpm), a peer-reviewed research journal (IJOVA), and professional associations locally has been so important in moving us forward as an profession (and quite honestly keeping some of us sane). That is why I recommended anyone just starting out in the field get connected to their local association and take advantage of any and all trainings regarding the key components of a well-run and professional volunteer resources manager."[18]

Susan Ellis thinks that volunteer management—at least how to partner with volunteers—should be taught as part of the professional curriculum for university degrees to people preparing for careers in the kinds of professions (social work, teaching, etc.) that often involve working with volunteers. "The fact that it's not mentioned, even though it's everywhere, the implication is either that there is nothing to say, or that it's so easy you ought to know how to do it by common sense, and both of those are wrong."[19]

The good news is that managing volunteers continues to be a critical function that contributes significantly to the success of volunteer-involving organizations. Ellis says: "There will always be volunteers, and when there are volunteers there will always be the need for leaders, because as it becomes more than five people in somebody's living room, it requires some management, so the need for leadership will never go away."[20] She says the profession will continue to evolve. "Whether we will begin to recognize it and value it, whether we'll stop making it the first job that gets laid off when the budgets are tight at the same time they then look for more volunteers, which is nothing if not contradictory, I do think we're always going to need the function. The function is not going to ever going to be obsolete. Ever."[21]

QUESTIONS TO GET YOU STARTED

1. What problems are you struggling with and where might you go to get help?
2. Are paid staff and volunteers working together in a cooperative way?
3. Which volunteers are you having problems with and what might you do to improve their effectiveness?
4. How might you raise the level of professionalism in your organization?
5. What resources would help you grow as a volunteer manager and improve your effectiveness?

CHAPTER 10

Resources, Support, and Information

INFORMATION ON VOLUNTEER MANAGEMENT

Blue Avocado blog: www.blueavocado.org, a free nonprofit online magazine for community nonprofits

Management Help: http://managementhelp.org, links to a wide range of articles and information

Charity Channel: http://charitychannel.com, a membership-based community for nonprofit professionals

Corporation for National and Community Service Resource Center: www.nationalserviceresources.org, a wide range of resources that includes online courses, effective practices, videos, and an online library

Energize, Inc. volunteer management resources: www.energizeinc .com, a wide range of resources, including articles, events, courses, free e-newsletter, bookstore

E-Volunteerism journal: www.e-volunteerism.com, a subscription-based electronic journal whose goal is to "inform and challenge volunteer leaders"

National Council of Nonprofits: http://www.councilofnonprofits.org/ resources/resources-topic/volunteers, information, tools, and sample documents

Service Leader nonprofit management program: www.serviceleader .org/leaders, specialized resources for volunteers, and managers of volunteers, operated by the RGK Center for Philanthropy and Community Service in the LBJ School of Public Affairs at The University of Texas at Austin

Urban Institute/National Center for Charitable Statistics: http://nccs .urban.org, surveys and statistics

Urban Institute: www.urban.org, research and policies

PRODUCTIVITY/COMMUNICATION

File Sharing/Collaboration

Online file-sharing works great for project collaboration and exchange of large files such as PowerPoint presentations, video clips, and photographs. There are also tools such as multi-user whiteboards and productivity applications such as desktop and document sharing. Here are a few of the options:

Apple iCloud: http://www.apple.com/icloud

Cx: https://www.cx.com

DeskAway: www.deskaway.com

Dropbox: www.dropbox.com

Evernote: www.evernote.com

Google Docs: www.docs.google.com

Huddle: www.huddle.com

Microsoft SkyDrive: http://windows.microsoft.com/en-US/skydrive/ home

Scribblar: www.scribblar.com

You Send It: www.yousendit.com

Free Conference Calls

Conference calls are great for committee or team collaboration by phone, or for simple meetings and decision making during periods of inclement weather or incompatible schedules. They are also helpful if you don't have a facility for holding meetings.

Free Conference Call: www.freeconferencecall.com

Go to Meeting: www.gotomeeting.com

Skype: www.skype.com

Online Calendars

Online calendars provide a way for multiple people to share the same calendar. You can use them to post meetings, project milestones and deadlines, or fundraising goals. You can also use them as a way for people to sign out equipment, reserve materials, sign up for work shifts, and anything else that is date-oriented. All are free but require registration by all participants.

Google: www.google.com/calendar

Hotmail: www.hotmail.com/calendar

Yahoo: www.yahoo.com/calendar

Templates, Forms, Planning Aids

Using existing forms and templates saves time and ensures you do not forget key elements. Most have been pretested. Planning aids provide process assistance as you work through your strategic or business planning process.

Business planning guide: http://web.sba.gov/busplantemplate/BizPlanStart.cfm

General business templates: www.myworktools.com

Miscellaneous templates: www.office.xerox.com/small-business-templates/enus.html

Online forms and surveys: www.formsite.com

Sample volunteer manual: http://solvehungertoday.org/GetInvolved/Volunteer/~/media/ILStCharles112/Files/PDF/GetInvolved/VolunteerManual2010.ashx

Strategic planning guide: http://socrates.berkeley.edu/~pbd/pdfs/Strategic_Planning.pdf

Volunteer management plan template: www.gladstone.qld.gov.au/c/document_library/get_file?uuid=2c772d61-1c30-4b61-a56c-9c50a4514ed7&groupId=1570002

Survey Tools

Online survey tools provide an easy way to conduct surveys. They allow you to create a survey and then email a link to participants. As participants respond, these tools tabulate the results automatically, allowing participants to remain anonymous (if you wish) and providing you with valuable information.

Key Survey: www.keysurvey.com

LimeSurvey: www.limesurvey.org

PollDaddy: www.polldaddy.com

QuestionPro: www.questionpro.com

SurveyGizmo: www.surveygizmo.com

Survey Monkey: www.surveymonkey.com

Zoomerang: www.zoomerang.com

E-Newsletters/Email Campaigns

These companies provide easy-to-use templates for creating mass emails, which can be structured in a newsletter format. The companies then email these communications using lists you provide.

Constant Contact: www.constantcontact.com

MailChimp: http://mailchimp.com

My Emma: http://myemma.com

Vertical Response: www.verticalresponse.com

BEST PRACTICES

Many organizations have their own best practices, but here are some good sources for general best practices that apply to nonprofit organizations:

Corporation for National & Community Service: www.nationalservice resources.org/effective-practice#effprac-by-topic

501 Commons: www.501commons.org/resources/tools-and-best -practices

Idealist: www.idealist.org/info/VolunteerMgmt/Best

Imagine Canada: library.imaginecanada.ca/resource_guides/volunteerism/ management

Managing Volunteers: A Good Practice Guide: www.citizens informationboard.ie/publications/providers/downloads/Managing _Volunteers_08.pdf

System for Adult Basic Education Support: http://www.sabes.org/administration/volunteer-management-training.pdf

The Urban Institute: www.urban.org/UploadedPDF/411005_Volunteer Management.pdf

University of San Diego: www.sandiego.edu/soles/centers/nonprofit/best_practice_library.php

Volunteer Bénévoles Yukon (Canada): www.volunteeryukon.ca/IMG/pdf/Best_Practices_Volunteer_Management.pdf

Volunteer Match: www.volunteermatch.org/nonprofits/learningcenter/

RECRUITING

If you need help attracting applicants for volunteer positions, here are some places in the United States where you can list job openings, including board positions:

Catch a Fire (professional skill matching): www.catchafire.org

ChristianVolunteering: www.christianvolunteering.org

Craigslist: www.craigslist.org

HandsOn Network: www.handsonnetwork.org

Idealist: www.Idealist.org

1-800 Volunteer.org: www.1-800-volunteer.org

ReServe: www.reserveinc.org

Sparked: http://www.sparked.com

United Way: www.Unitedway.org

Volunteer Match: www.Volunteermatch.org

Youth Service America: www.Servenet.org

SOFTWARE/CLOUD/ONLINE SYSTEMS

Big Tent: www.bigtent.com

Cervis Technologies: www.cervistech.com

CiviCore: www.civicore.com

Closerware: www.volunteermatters.com

Convio (Blackbaud): www.convio.com/common-ground/features/volunteer-management.html

HandsOn Connect: www.handsonconnect.org

VolunteerOnline: www.ivolunteer.com

Samaritan Technologies: http://samaritan.com

Shiftboard: www.shiftboard.com

SignUp Genius: www.signupgenius.com/index.cfm

Volgistics: www.volgistics.com

Volunteer Hub: www.volunteerhub.com

Volunteer IMPACT: www.volunteer2.com

Volunteer Matrix: http://volunteermatrix.com

Volunteer Matters: www.volunteermatters.com

Volunteer Reporter: http://volsoft.com

Volunteer Scheduler Pro: www.rotundasoftware.com/volunteers chedulerpro

VolunteerSpot: www.volunteerspot.com

WhenToHelp: http://whentohelp.com

YourVolunteers: http://yourvolunteers.com

Lists of Volunteer Management Software Sources

A Consumers Guide to Software for Volunteer Management (idealware): www.idealware.org/volunteer_management

Coyote Communications: www.coyotecommunications.com/tech/volmanage.html

Searchable List: www.manage-volunteers.org

LIABILITY/RISK MANAGEMENT

National Institute for Occupational Safety and Health: www.cdc.gov/niosh

Nonprofit Risk Management Center: http://nonprofitrisk.org

U.S. Department of Labor Occupational Safety and Health Administration: http://www.osha.gov

PROFESSIONAL ORGANIZATIONS, EDUCATION, CREDENTIALING, AND NETWORKING

AL!VE: Association of Leaders in Volunteer Engagement: www .volunteeralive.org

Alliance for Nonprofit Management: www.allianceonline.org

Association for Research on Nonprofit Organizations and Voluntary Action: www.arnova.org

Association for Volunteer Administration (AVA): see below under Directors of Volunteers in Agencies

Bridgestar: www.bridgestar.org/Home.aspx

Center for Association Leadership: www.asaecenter.org

Community Associations Institute: www.caionline.org

Council for Certification in Volunteer Administration: www.cvacert .org

CyberVPM: www.groups.yahoo.com/group/cybervpm

Directors of Volunteers in Agencies (DOVIA), Association for Volunteer Administrators (AVA), and other professional networks for those who coordinate volunteers: Each local or state organization has its own website

LinkedIn: www.linkedin.com

National Association of Volunteer Programs in Local Government: www.navplg.org

National Council of Nonprofits: www.councilofnonprofits.org

National Human Services Assembly Volunteerism Development Council: www.nassembly.org/Collaborations/PeerNetworks/ NOVN.aspx

National Organizations Volunteerism Network (NOVN): www .nassembly.org/Collaborations/PeerNetworks/NOVN.aspx

National Voluntary Organizations Active in Disaster (NVOAD): http:// www.nvoad.org

State associations of nonprofit organizations (Louisiana: www.lano .org, Pennsylvania: www.pano.org, Texas: www.tano.org, etc.)

Volunteer Management Group: www.volunteermanagementgroup.com

INTERNATIONAL RESOURCES

Asia

Asia Catalyst: http://asiacatalyst.org

Canada

Canadian Administrators of Volunteer Resources/Administrateurs canadiens des ressources bénévoles (CAVR): www.cavrcanada.org

Charity Village: www.charityvillage.com

Volunteer Canada, Canada's site for information on volunteering (in English and French): www.volunteer.ca

Ireland

Volunteer Ireland: http://www.volunteer.ie

Mexico

Centro Mexicano para la Filantropia: www.cemefi.org

United Kingdom

Association of Voluntary Services Managers: www.avsm.org.uk

VolResource: www.volresource.org.uk

Volunteering England: www.volunteering.org.uk

Volunteer Development Scotland: www.vds.org.uk

Volunteer Now (Northern Ireland): www.volunteering-ni.org

Wales Council for Voluntary Action: www.wcva.org.uk

Yahoo Group: http://groups.yahoo.com/group/ukvpms

Australia

Government of Western Australia Department of Sport and Recreation: http://www.dsr.wa.gov.au/resources

Volunteering Australia: www.volunteeringaustralia.org

Volunteer Management Plan Workbook: www.ausport.gov.au/__data/ assets/pdf_file/0007/334951/Volunteer_Management_Plan_Work book.pdf

INFORMATION FOR VOLUNTEERS

There are thousands of organizations that are looking for volunteers. Here is a short list of some sites that have information on volunteering or links to volunteer opportunities.

General

HandsOn Network Volunteer Center: www.handsonnetwork.org

Idealist: www.idealist.org

Points of Light Institute: www.pointsoflight.org

Volunteer Match: www.volunteermatch.org

Volunteers of America: www.voa.org

Youth

Dosomething.org: www.dosomething.org

Opp-Guide to Community Service: www.opp-guide.com

Youth Activism Project: http://youthactivismproject.org

Youth Service America: www.ysa.org

Youth Volunteer Corps: http://yvca.org

Global

American Red Cross: www.redcross.org

Australasian Volunteer Program Management (OZVPM): www.ozvpm .com

Cross-Cultural Solutions: www.crossculturalsolutions.org

The International Association for Volunteer Effort: www.iave.org

Global Crossroad: www.globalcrossroad.com

Global Service Corps: www.globalservicecorps.org

Global Volunteer Network: www.globalvolunteernetwork.org

Global Volunteers: www.globalvolunteers.org

Lattitude: www.lattitude.org.au; www.lattitude.org.uk

Save the Children: www.savethechildren.org

United Nations: www.unv.org

Volunteer Global: http://volunteerglobal.com

Women on the Road: www.women-on-the-road.com/faith-based
-volunteering.html

World Alliance for Citizen Participation: www.civicus.org

World Volunteer Web: www.worldvolunteerweb.org

Faith-Based

American Jewish World Service: http://ajws.org

Catholic Volunteer Network: www.catholicvolunteernetwork.org

Christian Volunteering: www.christianvolunteering.org

Islamic Relief USA: www.irusa.org/volunteer

Mercy Volunteer Corps: www.mercyvolunteers.org

Microvolunteering

Help from Home: http://helpfromhome.org

Koodonation: www.koodonation.com

Microtareas (Spanish): www.microtareas.com

Sparked: www.sparked.com

VolunteerGuide: www.volunteerguide.org

Other

What type of volunteer are you (quiz)? www.getinvolved.ca/vquiz/english

SPECIALIZED GROUPS

Animal Care

Animal Sheltering Volunteer Management: www.animalsheltering.org/
resources/all-topics/volunteer-management.html

Volunteer Management for Animal Care Organizations: www.humane
society.org/assets/pdfs/hsp/volunteer.pdf

Corporate

CorpsGiving: www.corpsgiving.com

Court-Appointed/Court-Mandated

Volunteering and Mandatory Community Service: http://volunteer.ca/content/volunteering-and-mandatory-community-service-discussion-paper

Faith-Based

Catholic Medical Mission Board: www.cmmb.org

Church Volunteer Central: www.churchvolunteercentral.com

Allaahuakbar.net: www.allaahuakbar.net/islamic_management/volunteerism_in_islam.htm

Toolkit Volunteering for Faith-Based Organizations and Congregations: www.serverhodeisland.org/Portals/0/Uploads/Documents/PDFs/FinalToolkit.pdf

UJA Federation of New York: www.ujafedny.org/volunteer-management

Children/Family

CIRCLE (The Center for Information and Research on Civic Learning and Engagement): www.civicyouth.org

Family Volunteers: www.thevolunteerfamily.org

School volunteers: www.theschoolvolunteer.org

Environmental

http://csiro.au/files/files/pi52.pdf

Library

Library volunteer job descriptions: www.literacynet.org/clv/resources/jobs

Library Volunteers: http://midhudson.org/funding/fundraising/volunteers.htm

Medical

Association of Healthcare Volunteer Resource Professionals: www.ahvrp.org

HealthCare Volunteer: www.healthcarevolunteer.com

Hospice: www.hospicevolunteerassociation.org

International Medical Volunteers Association: www.imva.org

Medical Reserve Corps: www.medicalreservecorps.gov

Museum

American Association for Museum Volunteers: www.aamv.org

Put Your Gloves On! Managing Volunteers in Museum Collections:
http://library2.jfku.edu/Museum_Studies/Put_Your_Gloves_On.pdf

Police/Fire

Centers for Disease Control and Prevention (CDC): www.cdc.gov/
phpr/capabilities/capability15.pdf

Fire Manager online scheduler: www.firemanager.net

Managing Volunteer Fire Fighters: http://www.vcos.org/wp-content/
uploads/2009/10/FLSAManual_Small.pdf

VolunteerFD.org: www.volunteerfd.org

Volunteers in Police Service: www.policevolunteers.org

Political

Local Victory: www.localvictory.com

Seniors and Baby Boomers

Capturing Baby Boomer Volunteers: www.morevolunteers.com/
resour05.htm

Elder Helpers: www.elderhelpers.org

Harnessing Baby Boomer's Experience: www.nationalservice
resources.org/initiative-boomers

Senior Corps: www.seniorcorps.gov

Spontaneous

Managing Spontaneous Disaster Volunteers: www.oregonvolunteers
.org/media/uploads/FayeStone_PowerPoint.pdf

Managing Spontaneous Volunteers in Times of Disaster: www.citizen
corps.gov/downloads/pdf/ManagingSpontaneousVolunteers.pdf

SPECIAL EVENTS/DAYS

Global Corporate Philanthropy Day

Building awareness of corporate-community partnerships and inspiring businesses to engage further in philanthropy. www.corporatephilanthropy .org/events/international-corporate-philanthropy-day.html

Global Youth Service Day (GYSD)

GYSD is the largest and longest-running service event in the world and the only major service event dedicated to youth. Children and youth between the ages of 5 and 25 work with community organizations, schools, and faith-based organizations to implement service projects. Many GYSD projects address the world's most critical issues, such as childhood health and well-being, civil rights, and environmental conservation. GYSD is organized by YSA (Youth Service America), an international leader in the youth service movement. http://gysd.org

International Volunteer Day

The International Volunteer Day for Economic and Social Development (IVD) was adopted by the UN General Assembly through Resolution A/ RES/40/212 on December 17, 1985. Since then, governments, the UN system, and civil society organizations have successfully joined volunteers around the world to celebrate the Day on December 5. IVD offers an opportunity for volunteer organizations and individual volunteers to make visible their contributions—at local, national, and international levels—to the achievement of the Millennium Development Goals. Over the years, rallies, parades, community volunteering projects, environmental awareness, free medical care, and advocacy campaigns have all featured prominently on IVD. www.worldvolunteerweb.org/intl-vol-day.html

Make a Difference Day

Make a Difference Day, the largest national day of helping others, is sponsored annually by *USA Weekend* magazine and its 800 carrier newspapers. Make a Difference Day takes place on the fourth Saturday in October each year. www.makeadifferenceday.com

Mandela Day

The overarching objective of Mandela Day is to inspire individuals to take action to help change the world for the better, and in doing so build a global movement for good. Ultimately, it seeks to empower communities everywhere. More than just a single day, the idea is for individuals and organizations to "Take Action; Inspire Change; Make Every Day a Mandela Day." www.mandeladay.com

Martin Luther King Day of Service

In 1994, Congress designated the Martin Luther King, Jr. federal holiday as a national day of service and charged the Corporation for National and Community Service with leading this effort. Taking place each year on the third Monday in January, the MLK Day of Service is the only federal holiday observed as a national day of service—a "day on, not a day off." http://mlkday.gov

Sewa Day

According to the organizers, Sewa is embedded in Indian traditions and is actively promoted by different cultures and faiths—as the core belief is the same—to sacrifice your time and resources for the benefit of others without wanting anything in return.

On Sewa Day, thousands of good-hearted people across the world come together to perform Sewa and experience the joy of giving in its truest sense. By participating in this collective endeavor, the organizers hope that the seeds of Sewa are watered so that acts of kindness and public service are performed more often. Sewa Day is a catalyst in making this happen. www.sewaday.org/home

World Kindness Week

World Kindness Week is dedicated to celebrating the little things we do for others. http://www.actsofkindness.org

NATIONAL AND OTHER GOVERNMENT SERVICE

AmeriCorps: www.americorps.gov

AmeriCorps Alums: www.americorpsalums.org

Corporation for National and Community Service: www.national service.gov

Peace Corps: www.peacecorps.org

Serve.gov: www.serve.gov

National Association of Volunteer Programs in Local Government: www.navplg.org

Corporation for National and Community Service: www.national service.gov

Learn and Serve America: www.learnandserve.gov

Senior Corps: www.seniorcorps.gov

Notes

INTRODUCTION

1. Susan Ellis (President of Energize, Inc.), interviewed July 30, 2012.

2. Kamila Czerwinska, "International Volunteer Day: Imagine a World without Volunteers," cafebabel.com, http://www.cafebabel.co.uk/article/27518/focus-volunteering-three-out-of-ten-europeans.html, February 12, 2008, accessed June 27, 2012.

3. Ibid.

4. *Volunteering in America 2011 Research Highlights* (Washington, DC: Corporation for National and Community Service, August 2011).

5. Urban Institute, "Quick Facts about Nonprofits," http://nccs.urban.org/statistics/quickfacts.cfm, accessed May 20, 2012.

6. *Bridging the Gap: Enriching the Volunteer Experience to Build a Better Future for Our Communities* (Volunteer Canada), http://www.volunteer.ca/files/Bridging_the_Gap_English.PDF, accessed May 21, 2012.

7. Urban Institute, *Volunteer Management Capacity in America's Charities and Congregations* (Washington, DC: Urban Institute, February 2004), 8.

8. Mark A. Hager and Jeffrey L. Brudney, *Balancing Act: The Challenges and Benefits of Volunteers* (Washington, DC: Urban Institute, December 2004), 1.

CHAPTER 1

1. Lynn Spreadbury (Partner Engagement Manager, Save the Children), interviewed August 17, 2012.

2. Mary Pat Knauss (Board President, Wings for Success), interviewed August 17, 2012.

3. Susan Ellis (President of Energize, Inc.), interviewed July 30, 2012.

4. Back on My Feet website, http://www.backonmyfeet.org, accessed September 28, 2012.

5. Human Rights Campaign website, http://www.hrc.org/the-hrc-story/about-us, accessed September 28, 2012.

6. The American Society of Nephrology website, http://www.asn-online.org/about/, accessed September 28, 2012.

7. Homeless Assistance Leadership Organization website, http://www.haloinc.org, accessed September 30, 2012.

8. Knauss, interviewed August 17, 2012.

9. Wings for Success website, http://www.wingsforsuccess.org/about-us/vision-framework, accessed September 30, 2012.

10. Knauss, interviewed August 17, 2012.

11. Jeffrey L. Brudney, "Preparing the Organization for Volunteers." In Connors, Tracy D., ed., *The Volunteer Management Handbook: Leadership Strategies for Success*, 2nd ed. (Hoboken, NJ: John Wiley & Sons, 2012), 78.

12. Brudney, "Preparing the Organization for Volunteers," 67.

13. Maureen K. Eccleston (Director, Volunteer Maryland), interviewed July 14, 2012.

14. David Eisner, Robert T. Grimm Jr., Shannon Maynard, & Susannah Washburn, "The New Volunteer Workforce," *Stanford Social Innovation Review*, Stanford, CA: Leland Stanford Jr. University, Winter 2009, 32.

15. Ibid., 34.

16. Ibid., 36.

17. Ellis, interviewed July 30, 2012.

18. Ellis, interviewed July 30, 2012.

19. Steve McCurley and Rick Lynch, *Volunteer Management: Mobilizing all the Resources of the Community* (Downers Grove, IL: Heritage Arts Publishing, 1996), 120–121.

20. *Capitalizing on Volunteers' Skills: Volunteering by Occupation in America* (Washington, DC: Corporation for National and Community Service, September 2008), 2.

21. Mark A. Hager and Jeffrey L. Brudney, *Balancing Act: The Challenges and Benefits of Volunteers* (Washington, DC: Urban Institute, December 2004), 1.

22. Ellis, interviewed July 30, 2012.

CHAPTER 2

1. BrainyQuote website, Mahatma Gandhi Quotes, http://www .brainyquote.com/quotes/authors/m/mahatma_gandhi_3.html, accessed November 15, 2012.

2. *Capitalizing on Volunteers' Skills: Volunteering by Occupation in America* (Washington, DC: Corporation for National and Community Service, September 2008).

3. Richard E. Boyatzis, *David C. McClelland: Biographical Statement and Synopsis of His Work* (Hay Group, August 15, 2000). http:// www.haygroup.com/downloads/my/David_McClelland.pdf, accessed May 9, 2012.

4. Maureen K. Eccleston (Director, Volunteer Maryland), interviewed July 14, 2012.

5. Jim Starr (Vice President of Volunteer Management, American Red Cross), interviewed June 28, 2012.

6. *Bridging the Gap: Enriching the Volunteer Experience to Build a Better Future for Our Communities* (Volunteer Canada), http://www .volunteer.ca/files/English_Research_Fact_Sheet_Bridging_the_Gap.pdf, accessed May 21, 2012.

7. BrainyQuote website, George S. Patton Quotes, http://www .brainyquote.com/quotes/authors/g/george_s_patton.html, accessed April 23, 2012.

8. *America's Senior Volunteers* (Washington, DC: Independent Sector, June 2000), 6.

9. Nadine Jalandoni and Keith Hume, *America's Family Volunteers* (Washington, DC: Independent Sector, 2001), 9.

10. Mark A. Hager and Jeffrey L. Brudney, *Volunteer Management Practices and Retention of Volunteers* (Washington, DC: Urban Institute, June 2004), 11.

11. Lynn Spreadbury (Partner Engagement Manager, Save the Children), interviewed August 17, 2012.

12. *Bridging the Gap: Enriching the Volunteer Experience to Build a Better Future for Our Communities* (Volunteer Canada), http://www

.volunteer.ca/files/Bridging_the_Gap_English.PDF, accessed May 21, 2012.

13. Jason Zigmont, "Bringing Members Back to the Fold," http://www.volunteerfd.org/recruitment/articles/245129, accessed July 7, 2012.

14. *America's Senior Volunteers*, 5.

15. Jalandoni and Hume, 11.

16. Marc A. Music and John Wilson, *Volunteers: A Social Profile* (Bloomington and Indianapolis: Indiana University Press, 2008), 55.

17. *America's Senior Volunteers* (Washington, DC: Independent Sector, June 2000), 6.

18. Ki Mae Heussner, "Bronx Zoo Cobra: Mia Is Famous Snake's New Name," April 7, 2011, http://abcnews.go.com/Technology/bronx-zoo-cobra-mia-famous-snakes/story?id=13319078#.T2sslxFtqSo, accessed March 22, 2012.

19. @BronxZoosCobra, http://twitter.com/#!/bronxzooscobra, accessed March 22, 2012.

20. VolunteerMatch website, http://www.volunteermatch.org/search/opp744514.jsp, accessed September 24, 2012.

CHAPTER 3

1. The Iwise Wisdom on Demand Blog, http://www.iwise.com/Peter_Schultz, accessed April 5, 2012.

2. Betsy McFarland, *Volunteer Management for Animal Care Organizations* (Washington, DC: Humane Society of the United States, 2005), 14–15.

3. Betsy Price, "New Realities Demand More Artful Solutions," *News Journal* (Wilmington, DE), July 31, 2011.

4. Mary Vaughan (Volunteer Coordinator for the MobileMed ministry of the Episcopal Church of the Ascension, Gaithersburg, MD), interviewed July 7, 2012.

5. Tia Milne (Volunteer Manager, Northern Illinois Food Bank, Geneva, IL), interviewed July 23, 2012.

6. Lynn Spreadbury (Partner Engagement Manager, Save the Children), interviewed August 17, 2012.

7. Dan Gabor (Regional Field Director, Organizing for America PA), interviewed July 16, 2012.

8. Owl RE, http://www.owlre.com/wordpress/wp-content/uploads/2008/01/factsheet_owlre_quotes.pdf, accessed July 13, 2012.

9. Independent Sector website, http://www.independentsector.org/volunteer_time, accessed September 30, 2012.

10. Tony Goodrow (Volunteer^2), interviewed June 29, 2012.

11. Goodrow, interviewed June 29, 2012.

12. Goodrow, interviewed June 29, 2012.

13. Goodrow, interviewed June 29, 2012.

14. Susan Ellis (President of Energize, Inc.), interviewed July 30, 2012.

CHAPTER 4

1. BrainyQuote website, Leadership Quotes, http://www.brainyquote .com/quotes/topics/topic_leadership.html, accessed July 17, 2012.

2. Linda-Darling Hammond et al. "How People Learn: Introduction to Learning Theories," *The Learning Classroom: Theory into Practice, A Telecourse for Teacher Education and Professional Development* (Stanford University 2001), http://www.stanford.edu/class/ed269/hplintrochapter.pdf, accessed August 11, 2012.

3. Dan Gabor (Regional Field Director for Organizing for America PA), interviewed July 16, 2012.

4. Jim Starr (Vice President of Volunteer Management, American Red Cross), interviewed June 28, 2012.

5. Meghan Kaskoun (Volunteer Manager, Aronoff Center for the Arts, Cincinnati Arts Association), interviewed June 26, 2012.

6. Betty Stallings and Donna McMillion, "Orientation and Training of Event Volunteers," *How to Produce Fabulous Fundraising Events*, 49–51, http://www.energizeinc.com/art/ahowt.html, accessed August 11, 2012.

7. Mary Pat Knauss (Board President, Wings for Success), interviewed August 17, 2012.

8. Gabor, interviewed July 16, 2012.

9. Starr, interviewed June 28, 2012.

10. Kaskoun, interviewed June 26, 2012.

11. Susan Ellis, "Susan's Tip of the Month: Connect Volunteers and Employees for Staff Development," *Energize Volunteer Management Update*, July 2012, http://archive.constantcontact.com/fs070/11011283469 60/archive/1110384950526.html#a5, accessed August 12, 2012.

12. Susan Ellis (President of Energize, Inc.), interviewed July 30, 2012.

CHAPTER 5

1. BrainyQuote website, Leadership Quotes, http://www.brainyquote .com/quotes/topics/topic_leadership.html, accessed July 17, 2012.

2. Susan Ellis (President of Energize, Inc.), interviewed July 30, 2012.

3. "How to Volunteer from Home," June 6, 2011, http://www.pitchin .org/how-to-volunteer-from-home.htm, accessed June 27, 2012.

4. Tony Goodrow (Volunteer^2), interviewed June 29, 2012.

5. ThinkExist website, James H. Boren Quotes, http://thinkexist.com/ quotation/when_in_doubt-mumble-when_in_trouble-delegate/7886.html, accessed April 14, 2012.

6. Dan Gabor (Regional Field Director, Organizing for America PA), interviewed July 16, 2012.

7. BrainyQuote website, Schedule Quotes, http://www.brainyquote .com/quotes/keywords/schedule.html?gclid=CMjhxKGQl7ECFYTd4Aod _DBvfw, accessed July 13, 2012.

8. Mary Vaughan (Volunteer Coordinator for the MobileMed ministry of the Episcopal Church of the Ascension, Gaithersburg, MD), interviewed July 7, 2012.

9. Jim Starr (Vice President of Volunteer Management, American Red Cross), interviewed June 28, 2012.

10. Sara Inés Calderón, "Obama Campaign Releases Mobile Voter Engagement App," TechCrunch, http://techcrunch.com/2012/07/31/ obama-campaign-releases-mobile-voter-engagement-app, accessed September 25, 2012.

11. Goodrow, interviewed June 29, 2012.

12. Goodrow, interviewed June 29, 2012.

13. BrainyQuote website, Leadership Quotes, http://www.brainy quote.com/quotes/topics/topic_leadership.html, accessed July 17, 2012.

CHAPTER 6

1. BrainyQuote website, Liability Quotes, http://www.brainyquote .com/quotes/keywords/liability.html, accessed October 3, 2012.

2. National Public Radio, *This American Life*, Episode 431: "See No Evil," originally aired April 1, 2011, http://www.thisamericanlife.org/ radio-archives/episode/431/transcript, accessed April 4, 2012.

3. Purdue University Policies, Human Resources, Volunteers, Interim (VI.B.2), http://www.purdue.edu/policies/human-resources/vib2.html, accessed September 25, 2012.

4. The Church of Jesus Christ Latter-Day Saints, "Political Neutrality," http://www.mormonnewsroom.org/official-statement/political-neutrality, accessed May 15, 2012.

5. Maureen K. Eccleston (Director, Volunteer Maryland), interviewed July 14, 2012.

6. Eccleston, interviewed July 14, 2012.

7. Volunteer Protection Act of 1997, Public Law 105-19, June 18, 1997, http://www.doi.ne.gov/shiip/volunteer/pl_105.19.pdf, accessed August 9, 2012.

8. Pfau England Nonprofit Law, P.C. website, "Volunteer Liability and the Volunteer Protection Act of 1997," *Nonprofit Quicktips*, http://www.nonprofitlaw.com/Default.aspx?pageId=1050140, accessed September 7, 2012.

9. "Managing Volunteers: Balancing Risk and Reward" (Santa Cruz, CA: Nonprofits' Insurance Alliance of California and the Alliance of Nonprofits for Insurance, 2000), 1–2.

10. Linda L. Graff. *Better Safe . . . : Risk Management in Volunteer Programs and Community Service* (Dundas, Ontario, Canada: Linda Graff and Associates, 2003), 2.

11. "Ryan Seacrest Profiles Michael Phelps," http://www.nbcolympics.com/video/swimming/ryan-seacrest-profiles-michael-phelps.html, accessed August 1, 2012.

CHAPTER 7

1. ThinkExist website, Vince Lombardi Quotes, http://thinkexist.com/quotation/individual_commitment_to_a_group_effort-that_is/15114.html, accessed October 3, 2012.

2. Nadine Jalandoni and Keith Hume, *America's Family Volunteers* (Washington, DC: Independent Sector, 2001), 2.

3. Jalandoni and Hume, *America's Family Volunteers*, 5.

4. Tia Milne (Volunteer Manager, Northern Illinois Food Bank, Geneva, IL), interviewed July 23, 2012.

5. Jalandoni and Hume, *America's Family Volunteers*, 10.

6. *Bridging the Gap: Enriching the Volunteer Experience to Build a Better Future for Our Communities* (Volunteer Canada), http://www.volunteer.ca/files/Bridging_the_Gap_English.PDF, accessed May 21, 2012.

7. Lori Gotlieb, "Corporate Partnerships: How We Need to Tap into This Rich Resource," Charity Village website, http://www.charityvillage.com/cv/research/rvol63.html, September 14, 2009, accessed April 4, 2012.

8. Red Emma, "Big Greenwashing 101," *Earth First! Newswire*, http://earthfirstnews.wordpress.com/articles/big-greenwashing-101/, accessed April 17, 2012.

9. Carole Sevilla Brown, "Angry Supporters Withdraw Donations to National Wildlife Federation to Protest Partnership with Scotts Miracle

Gro," Ecosystem Gardening website, http://www.ecosystemgardening .com/angry-supporters-withdraw-donations-to-national-wildlife-federation -to-protest-partnership-with-scotts-miracle-gro.html, accessed April 17, 2012.

10. Milne, interviewed July 23, 2012.

11. Lynn Spreadbury (Partner Engagement Manager, Save the Children), interviewed August 17, 2012.

12. UPS Corporate Responsibility website, "Our Mission," http:// www.community.ups.com/UPS+Foundation, accessed April 4, 2012.

13. Ronna Charles Branch (UPS Global Reputation Management PR Supervisor), interviewed January 13, 2012.

14. *Bridging the Gap* (Volunteer Canada), http://www.volunteer.ca/ files/Bridging_the_Gap_English.PDF.

15. Milne, interviewed July 23, 2012.

16. Independent Sector. *Engaging in Lifelong Service: Findings and Recommendations for Encouraging a Tradition of Voluntary Action Among America's Youth* (Washington, DC: Independent Sector, 2002), 6.

17. *Bridging the Gap* (Volunteer Canada), http://www.volunteer.ca/ files/Bridging_the_Gap_English.PDF.

18. Jim Starr (Vice President of Volunteer Management, American Red Cross), interviewed June 28, 2012.

19. Ronna Charles Branch, interviewed January 13, 2012.

20. Meghan Kaskoun (Volunteer Manager, Aronoff Center for the Arts, Cincinnati Arts Association), interviewed June 26, 2012.

21. Milne, interviewed July 23, 2012.

22. Kaskoun, interviewed June 26, 2012.

23. Starr, interviewed June 28, 2012.

24. The National Association of Colleges and Employers, "Intern Hiring Up 8.5 Percent," http://www.naceweb.org/Press/Releases/Intern _Hiring_Up_8_5_Percent.aspx?referal=pressroom&menuid=273, accessed August 3, 2012.

25. Ross Perlin. *Intern Nation: How to Earn Nothing and Learn Little in the Brave New Economy* (London and New York: Verso, 2011).

26. Steven Greenhouse, "Jobs Few, Grads Flock to Unpaid Internships," *New York Times*, May 5, 2012, http://www.nytimes.com/2012/05/06/ business/unpaid-internships-dont-always-deliver.html?pagewanted=all, accessed August 3, 2012.

27. Intern Bridge, "Is Your Internship Program in Compliance with Federal Law?" http://www.internbridge.com/white/files/comp.pdf, accessed August 3, 2012.

28. U.S. Department of Labor, http://www.dol.gov/elaws/esa/flsa/docs/trainees.asp, accessed August 3, 2012.

29. Susan J. Ellis, "Interns: The 'Acceptable' Volunteers?" *Hot Topics*, November 2004, Energize.com website, http://www.energizeinc.com/hot/2004/04nov.html, accessed August 3, 2012.

30. *Keeping Baby Boomers Volunteering: A Research Brief on Volunteer Retention and Turnover, Executive Summary* (Washington, DC: Corporation for National and Community Service, March 2007).

31. *Baby Boomers and Volunteering: An Analysis of the Current Population Survey* (Washington, DC: Corporation for National and Community Service, December 2005).

32. *Keeping Baby Boomers*, 3.

33. *Bridging the Gap* (Volunteer Canada), http://www.volunteer.ca/files/Bridging_the_Gap_English.PDF.

34. Kaskoun, interviewed June 26, 2012.

35. Barbara A. Butrica, Richard W. Johnson, and Sheila R. Zedlewski, *Volunteer Transitions among Older Americans* (Washington, DC: Urban Institute, October 2007) 2.

36. Kaskoun, interviewed June 26, 2012.

37. Independent Sector. *America's Senior Volunteers*, 7.

38. Matthew W. Brault, "Americans with Disabilities: 2010," *Current Population Reports*, U.S. Census Bureau, July 2012, http://www.census.gov/prod/2012pubs/p70-131.pdf, accessed September 28, 2012.

39. Koodoonation website, http://koodo.koodo.sparked.com/content/learnkoodo, accessed May 21, 2012.

40. Konstantinos Tomazos and Richard Butler, "Volunteer Tourism: The New Ecotourism?" *Anatolia, 20*, no. 1(2009): 196–212. http://strathprints.strath.ac.uk/16612/1/strathprints016612.pdf, accessed June 19, 2012.

41. Cheryle N. Yallen, "Assessment, Planning, and Staffing Analysis," in Tracy D. Connors, ed., *The Volunteer Management Handbook: Leadership Strategies for Success*, 2nd ed. (Hoboken: John Wiley & Sons, 2012), 132.

42. Starr, interviewed June 28, 2012.

CHAPTER 8

1. Steven R. Covey, *The 7 Habits of Highly Effective People* (New York: Free Press, 2004), 241.

2. Steve McCurley and Rick Lynch, *Volunteer Management: Mobilizing all the Resources of the Community* (Downers Grove, IL: Heritage Arts Publishing, 1996), 121.

3. Lynn Spreadbury (Partner Engagement Manager, Save the Children), interviewed August 17, 2012.

4. *Keeping Baby Boomers Volunteering: A Research Brief on Volunteer Retention and Turnover, Executive Summary* (Washington, DC: Corporation for National and Community Service, March 2007), 3.

5. *Bridging the Gap: Enriching the Volunteer Experience to Build a Better Future for Our Communities* (Volunteer Canada), http://www.volunteer.ca/files/English_Research_Fact_Sheet_Bridging_the_Gap.pdf, accessed May 21, 2012.

6. Susan M. Heathfield, "Inspirational Quotes for Business: Empowerment and Delegation," http://humanresources.about.com/od/workrelationships/a/quotes_empower.htm, accessed April 14, 2012.

7. Jim Starr (Vice President of Volunteer Management, American Red Cross), interviewed June 28, 2012.

8. Cynthia Myers, personal communication.

9. SimplyPsychology website, http://www.simplypsychology.org/maslow.html, accessed November 19, 2012.

10. Jason Zigmont, "Bringing Members Back to the Fold," VolunteerFd.org website, http://www.volunteerfd.org, http://www.volunteerfd.org/recruitment/articles/245129, accessed July 7, 2012.

11. Barbara A. Butrica, Richard W. Johnson, and Sheila R. Zedlewski, "Retaining Older Volunteers Is Key to Meeting Future Volunteer Needs," *The Retirement Project: Perspectives on Productive Aging* (Washington, DC: Urban Institute, December 2007).

12. Mary Vaughan (Volunteer Coordinator for the MobileMed ministry of the Episcopal Church of the Ascension, Gaithersburg, MD), interviewed July 7, 2012.

13. Tia Milne (Volunteer Manager, Northern Illinois Food Bank, Geneva, IL), interviewed July 23, 2012.

14. James C. Fisher and Kathleen M. Cole, *Leadership and Management of Volunteer Programs: A Guide for Volunteer Administrators* (San Francisco: Jossey-Bass, 1993), 71.

15. Gary Chapman and Paul White, *The 5 Languages of Appreciation in the Workplace: Empowering Organizations by Encouraging People* (Chicago: Northfield, 2011).

16. Tia Milne, interviewed July 23, 2012.

17. Vaughan, interviewed July 7, 2012.

18. Dan Gabor (Regional Field Director, Organizing for America PA), interviewed July 16, 2012.

19. Starr, interviewed June 28, 2012.

20. Milne, interviewed July 23, 2012.

CHAPTER 9

1. BrainyQuote website, Problems Quotes, http://www.brainyquote .com/quotes/keywords/problems.html, accessed July 17, 2012.

2. Susan J. Ellis, "Common Sense and Volunteer Involvement," April 2012, http://www.energizeinc.com/hot/2012/12apr.php, accessed August 10, 2012.

3. Mary Vaughan (Volunteer Coordinator for the MobileMed ministry at the Episcopal Church of the Ascension, Gaithersburg, MD), interviewed July 7, 2012.

4. The Quote Garden website, Quotations about Leadership, http:// www.quotegarden.com/leadership.html, accessed May 31, 2012.

5. Maureen K. Eccleston (Director, Volunteer Maryland), interviewed July 14, 2012.

6. Tony Goodrow (Founder of Volunteer[2]), interviewed June 29, 2012.

7. Mary Vaughan, interviewed July 7, 2012.

8. Meghan Kaskoun (Volunteer Manager, Aronoff Center for the Arts, Cincinnati Arts Association), interviewed June 26, 2012.

9. Tony Goodrow, interviewed June 29, 2012.

10. Tia Milne (Volunteer Manager, Northern Illinois Food Bank, Geneva, IL), interviewed July 23, 2012.

11. Tony Goodrow, interviewed June 29, 2012.

12. Ronna Charles Branch (UPS Global Reputation Management PR Supervisor), interviewed January 13, 2012.

13. Maureen K. Eccleston, interviewed July 14, 2012.

14. Meghan Kaskoun, interviewed June 26, 2012.

15. Maureen K. Eccleston, interviewed July 14, 2012.

16. Tony Goodrow, interviewed June 29, 2012.

17. Meghan Kaskoun, interviewed June 26, 2012.

18. Meghan Kaskoun, personal communication, June 27, 2012.

19. Susan Ellis (President of Energize, Inc.), interviewed July 30, 2012.

20. Susan Ellis, interviewed July 30, 2012.

21. Susan Ellis, interviewed July 30, 2012.

Bibliography

Battle, Richard V. *The Volunteer Handbook: How to Organize and Manage a Successful Organization.* Austin, TX: Volunteer Concepts, 1988.

Brudney, Jeffrey L. "Preparing the Organization for Volunteers." In *The Volunteer Management Handbook: Leadership Strategies for Success,* 2nd ed., edited by Connors, Tracy D. Hoboken, NJ: John Wiley & Sons, 2012.

Butrica, Barbara A., Richard W. Johnson, and Sheila R. Zedlewski. "Retaining Older Volunteers Is Key to Meeting Future Volunteer Needs." *The Retirement Project: Perspectives on Productive Aging.* Washington, DC: Urban Institute, December 2007.

Butrica, Barbara A., Richard W. Johnson, and Sheila R. Zedlewski. "Volunteer Transitions among Older Americans." *Retirement Project: Discussion Paper Series.* Washington, DC: Urban Institute, October 2007.

Calderón, Sara Inés. "Obama Campaign Releases Mobile Voter Engagement App." TechCrunch, http://techcrunch.com/2012/07/31/obama-campaign-releases-mobile-voter-engagement-app, accessed September 25, 2012.

Chapman, Gary, and Paul White. *The 5 Languages of Appreciation in the Workplace: Empowering Organizations by Encouraging People.* Chicago: Northfield Publishing, 2011.

Citizens Information Board. *Managing Volunteers: A Good Practice Guide.* Dublin, Ireland: Citizens Information Board, 2008. http://

www.citizensinformationboard.ie/publications/providers/ downloads/Managing_Volunteers_08.pdf, accessed September 29, 2012.

Connors, Tracy D., ed. *The Volunteer Management Handbook: Leadership Strategies for Success*, 2nd ed. Hoboken, NJ: John Wiley & Sons, 2012.

Corporation for National and Community Service. *Baby Boomers and Volunteering: An Analysis of the Current Population Survey*. Washington, DC: Corporation for National and Community Service, December 2005.

Corporation for National and Community Service. *Capitalizing on Volunteers' Skills: Volunteering by Occupation in America*. Washington, DC: Corporation for National and Community Service, September 2008.

Corporation for National and Community Service. *Keeping Baby Boomers Volunteering: A Research Brief on Volunteer Retention and Turnover, Executive Summary*. Washington, DC: Corporation for National and Community Service, March 2007.

Corporation for National and Community Service. *Volunteering in America 2011: Research Highlights*. Washington, DC: Corporation for National and Community Service, August 2011.

Czerwinska, Kamila. "International Volunteer Day: Imagine a World without Volunteers." cafebabel.com, http://www.cafebabel.co.uk/ article/27518/focus-volunteering-three-out-of-ten-europeans.html (February 12, 2008), accessed June 27, 2012.

Driggers, Preston, and Eileen Dumas. *Managing Library Volunteers*, 2nd ed. Chicago: American Library Association, 2011.

Eisner, David, Robert T. Grimm Jr., Shannon Maynard, and Susannah Washburn. "The New Volunteer Workforce," *Stanford Social Innovation Review*. Stanford, CA: Leland Stanford Jr. University, Winter 2009, 32–37.

Ellis, Susan J. "Common Sense and Volunteer Involvement," April 2012, http://www.energizeinc.com/hot/2012/12apr.php, accessed August 10, 2012.

Ellis, Susan J. "Interns: The 'Acceptable' Volunteers?" Hot Topics, November 2004, Energize.com, http://www.energizeinc.com/hot/ 2004/04nov.html, accessed August 3, 2012.

Ellis, Susan J. "Susan's Tip of the Month: Connect Volunteers and Employees for Staff Development," *Energize Volunteer Management Update*, July 2012, http://archive.constantcontact.com/fs070/

1101128346960/archive/1110384950526.html#a5, accessed August 12, 2012.

Ellis, Susan J. "Why Do We Love Volunteer Satisfaction Surveys?" Hot Topics June, 2012, Energize.com, http://www.energizeinc.com/hot/2012/12jun.php, accessed September 28, 2012.

Fisher, James C., and Kathleen M. Cole. *Leadership and Management of Volunteer Programs: A Guide for Volunteer Administrators.* San Francisco: Jossey-Bass, 1993.

Federal Emergency Management Agency (FEMA). *Developing and Managing Volunteers* (Independent Study). Emmitsburg, MD: FEMA, February 2006, http://training.fema.gov/emiweb/downloads/IS244.pdf, accessed September 29, 2012.

Fixler, Jill Friedman, Sandie Eichberg, and Gail Lorenz. *Boomer Volunteer Engagement: Collaborate Today, Thrive Tomorrow.* Breinigsville, PA: Turner Publishing, 2009.

Gay, Kathlyn. *Volunteering: The Ultimate Teen Guide.* Lanham, MD: Scarecrow Press, 2004.

Gotlieb, Lori. "Corporate Partnerships: How We Need to Tap into This Rich Resource." http://www.charityvillage.com/cv/research/rvol63.html, September 14, 2009, accessed April 4, 2012.

Graff, Linda L. *Better Safe . . . : Risk Management in Volunteer Programs and Community Service.* Dundas, Ontario, Canada: Linda Graff and Associates, 2003.

Graff, Linda L. *By Definition: Policies for Volunteer Programs.* Hamilton, Ontario, Canada: Graff and Associates, 1997.

Greenhouse, Steven, "Jobs Few, Grads Flock to Unpaid Internships," *New York Times*, May 5, 2012, http://www.nytimes.com/2012/05/06/business/unpaid-internships-dont-always-deliver.html?pagewanted=all, accessed August 3, 2012.

Hager, Mark A., and Jeffrey L. Brudney. *Balancing Act: The Challenges and Benefits of Volunteers.* Washington, DC: Urban Institute, December 2004.

Hager, Mark A., and Jeffrey L. Brudney. *Volunteer Management Practices and Retention of Volunteers.* Washington, DC: Urban Institute, June 2004.

Hammond, Linda-Darling, Kim Austin, Suzanne Orcutt, and Jim Rosso. "How People Learn: Introduction to Learning Theories," *The Learning Classroom: Theory into Practice*, A Telecourse for Teacher Education and Professional Development, Stanford University 2001. http://www.stanford.edu/class/ed269/hplintrochapter.pdf, accessed August 11, 2012.

HandsOn Network. *Starting a Volunteer Program*. Atlanta, GA: HandsOn Network, 2010.

Hoyt, Hannah. "Inequality and Unpaid Labor," *Dartmouth*, May 30, 2012, http://thedartmouth.com/2012/05/30/opinion/hoyt, accessed August 3, 2012.

Independent Sector. *America's Senior Volunteers*. Washington, DC: Independent Sector, June 2000.

Independent Sector. *Engaging in Lifelong Service: Findings and Recommendations for Encouraging a Tradition of Voluntary Action Among America's Youth*. Washington, DC: Independent Sector, 2002.

Independent Sector. *Measuring Volunteering: A Practical Toolkit*. Washington, DC: Independent Sector, 2001.

Intern Bridge. "Is Your Internship Program in Compliance with Federal Law?" http://www.internbridge.com/white/files/comp.pdf, accessed August 3, 2012.

Jalandoni, Nadine, and Keith Hume. *America's Family Volunteers*. Washington, DC: Independent Sector, 2001.

Lipp, John L. *The Complete Idiot's Guide to Recruiting and Managing Volunteers*. New York: Penguin Group, 2009.

MacLeod, Flora. *Motivating and Managing Today's Volunteers*. British Columbia, Canada: International Self-Counsel Press, 1993.

McCurley, Steve, and Rick Lynch. *Volunteer Management: Mobilizing All the Resources of the Community*. Downers Grove, IL: Heritage Arts Publishing, 1996.

McFarland, Betsy. *Volunteer Management for Animal Care Organizations*. Washington, DC: Humane Society of the United States, 2005.

McNamara, Carter. "Developing and Managing Volunteer Programs," Management Help, http://managementhelp.org/staffing/volunteers.htm, accessed August 31, 2012.

Moore, Danielle, and Stephanie Fishlock, *Can Do! Volunteering: A Guide to Involving Young Disabled People as Volunteers*. London, UK: Leonard Cheshire/Scope, 2006, http://www.scope.org.uk/sites/default/files/pdfs/Volunteering/can_do_it_volunteering_toolkit.pdf, accessed September 28, 2012.

Music, Marc A., and John Wilson. *Volunteers: A Social Profile*. Bloomington and Indianapolis: Indiana University Press, 2008.

The National Association of Colleges and Employers. "Intern Hiring Up 8.5 Percent," http://www.naceweb.org/Press/Releases/Intern_Hiring_Up

_8_5_Percent.aspx?referal=pressroom&menuid=273, accessed August 3, 2012.

The Nonprofits' Insurance Alliance of California and the Alliance of Non-profits for Insurance. "Managing Volunteers: Balancing Risk and Reward," Santa Cruz, CA: The Nonprofits' Insurance Alliance of California and the Alliance of Nonprofits for Insurance, 2000.

Nonprofit HR Solutions. *2012 Nonprofit Employment Trends Survey.* Washington, DC: Nonprofit HR Solutions, 2012.

Nonprofit Research Collaborative. *November 2010 Fundraising Survey.* Vancouver, British Columbia, Canada: The Nonprofit Research Collaborative, 2010.

Ott, J. Steven, and Lisa A. Dicke, eds. *Understanding Nonprofit Organizations: Governance, Leadership, and Management*, 2nd ed. Boulder, CO: Westview Press, 2012.

Patterson, John C. "Does Liability for Negligent Hiring Apply to Volunteers?" *Staff Screening Tool Kit*, 13–14, http://www.energizeinc.com/art/asta.html, accessed July 30, 2012.

Perlin, Ross. *Intern Nation: How to Earn Nothing and Learn Little in the Brave New Economy.* London and New York: Verso, 2011.

Pfau England Nonprofit Law, P.C. website, "Volunteer Liability and the Volunteer Protection Act of 1997," Nonprofit Quicktips, http://www.nonprofitlaw.com/Default.aspx?pageId=1050140, accessed September 7, 2012.

Price, Betsy. "New Realities Demand More Artful Solutions," *News Journal* (Wilmington, DE), July 31, 2011.

Red Emma. "Big Greenwashing 101," *Earth First! Newswire*, http://earthfirstnews.wordpress.com/articles/big-greenwashing-101/, accessed April 17, 2012.

Rigby, Ben. "Why Microvolunteering Is Not Virtual Volunteering," Sparked Blog, December 24, 2010, http://blog.beextra.org/2010/12/why-microvolunteering-is-not-virtual-volunteering.html, accessed September 29, 2012.

Salamon, Lester M., and Kasey L. Spence. *Volunteers and the Economic Downturn.* Washington, DC: Corporation for National and Community Service, July 2009.

Spiro, Josh, "How to Manage Interns," April 22, 2010, http://www.inc.com/guides/2010/04/managing-interns.html, accessed August 3, 2012.

Stallings, Betty, and Donna McMillion, "Orientation and Training of Event Volunteers," *How to Produce Fabulous Fundraising Events*, 49–51, http://www.energizeinc.com/art/ahowt.html, accessed August 11, 2012.

Tomazos, Konstantinos, and Richard Butler. "Volunteer Tourism: The New Ecotourism?" *Anatolia,* 20, no. 1 (2009), 196–212, http://strathprints.strath.ac.uk/16612/1/strathprints016612.pdf, accessed June 19, 2012.

U.S. Department of Labor. "Trainees," *eLaws Fair Labor Standards Act Advisor.* http://www.dol.gov/elaws/esa/flsa/docs/trainees.asp, accessed August 3, 2012.

Urban Institute. *Quick Facts about Nonprofits.* Washington, DC: National Center for Charitable Statistics, 2012, http://nccs.urban.org/statistics/quickfacts.cfm, accessed May 20, 2012.

Urban Institute. *Volunteer Management Capacity in America's Charities and Congregations.* Washington, DC: Urban Institute, February 2004.

Volunteer Canada. *Bridging the Gap: Enriching the Volunteer Experience to Build a Better Future for Our Communities.* Volunteer Canada, www.volunteer.ca/study, accessed May 21, 2012.

Volunteer Canada. *Rethinking Volunteer Engagement.* Volunteer Canada, 2001, http://volunteer.ca/files/RethinkingEng.pdf, accessed September 29, 2012.

Volunteering Australia, Involving Volunteers with a Disability (Subject Guide), 2006, http://www.volunteeringaustralia.org/files/FZDEJFZ26O/VOLU_Disibility_Section4_FINAL_2_.pdf, accessed September 28, 2012.

Volunteer Protection Act of 1997, Public Law 105-19, June 18, 1997, http://www.doi.ne.gov/shiip/volunteer/pl_105.19.pdf, accessed August 9, 2012.

Yallen, Cheryle N. "Assessment, Planning, and Staffing Analysis," *The Volunteer Management Handbook: Leadership Strategies for Success*, 2nd ed., edited by Tracy D. Connors. Hoboken, NJ: John Wiley & Sons, 2012.

Zigmont, Jason. "Bringing Members Back to the Fold," http://www.volunteerfd.org/recruitment/articles/245129, accessed July 7, 2012.

INTERVIEW SOURCES

Ronna Charles Branch, UPS Global Reputation Management PR Supervisor, interviewed January 13, 2012.

Maureen K. Eccleston, Director, Volunteer Maryland, interviewed July 14, 2012.

Susan Ellis, President of Energize, Inc., interviewed July 30, 2012.

Dan Gabor, Regional Field Director, Organizing for America PA, interviewed July 16, 2012.

Tony Goodrow, Founder of Volunteer^2, interviewed June 29, 2012.

Meghan Kaskoun, Volunteer Manager, Aronoff Center for the Arts, Cincinnati Arts Association, interviewed June 26, 2012.

Mary Pat Knauss, Board President, Wings for Success, interviewed August 17, 2012.

Tia Milne, Volunteer Manager, Northern Illinois Food Bank, Geneva, IL, interviewed July 23, 2012.

Lynn Spreadbury, Partner Engagement Manager, Save the Children, interviewed August 17, 2012.

Jim Starr, Vice President of Volunteer Management, American Red Cross, interviewed June 28, 2012.

Mary Vaughan, Volunteer Coordinator for the MobileMed ministry of the Episcopal Church of the Ascension, Gaithersburg, MD, interviewed July 7, 2012.

Index

About the Author

Nancy Sakaduski is a professional marketing consultant who, through her company Sakaduski Marketing Solutions, helps businesses and organizations grow and succeed. She has also worked directly with many nonprofit organizations, including Penn State Master Gardeners, the Northport Historical Society, and the Center for the Creative Arts. The author's background includes business education, business experience (including managing staff), and volunteer management. This combination provides a good vantage point for bringing effective business techniques to the real-world challenges of managing volunteer workforces. She is the author of sixteen books, the most recent of which was *Scientific English: A Guide for Scientists and Other Professionals*, which she co-authored with her father, Robert A. Day. She holds an Executive MBA from Loyola University in Baltimore.